blood AND MILK

a novel in stories

BLOOD AND MILK

A Novel in Stories

W. D. BLACKMON

et alia press

LITTLE ROCK, ARKANSAS
2011

www.etaliapress.com

Copyright © 2011 W. D. Blackmon

Published in the United States of America by
Et Alia Press
5001 Woodlawn Drive
Little Rock, AR 72205

ISBN 978-0-9828184-2-8
Library of Congress Control Number: 2011924365

Cover Design: Jesse Nickles
Text Design: Angelia Northrip-Rivera

Photographs by Julie Blackmon
  Cover and page 6: "Broken Toy" (detail)
  Page 28: "Naptime"
  Page 48: "Time Out"
  Page 72: "PC" (detail)
  Page 94: "Green Velvet" (detail)

Contents

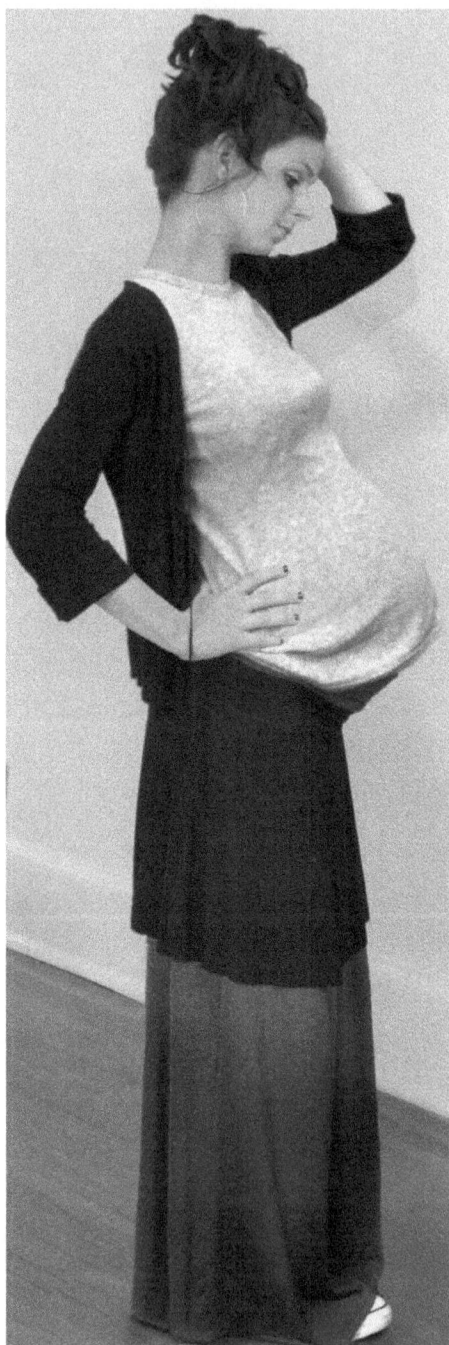

BLOOD AND MILK

Becky Hawkins noticed that she was the only one in the five active check-out lines at the Kroger Super Center who was nine months pregnant and caring for an eighty-six-year-old grandfather and six-year-old brain-injured child. She had been proud of the way she was handling this nearly impossible challenge until about two seconds before, when her grandfather grabbed a KitKat bar from a startled little boy behind them in line and said, "That's mine, you little bastard!" in a very hateful and threatening tone.

"Granddad," Becky said, not missing a beat, "I think you're mistaken. *This* is *your* KitKat bar." Squatting with great effort, she picked up a bar from a low shelf of the candy display case. "Here, honey. Give that boy back his candy," she said authoritatively.

Amazing luck. He gave the candy back with a smug gallantry that suggested he'd thought of this whole clever scenario, but when he turned away from the shocked boy's family, there was a stunned look on his face. He whispered to himself so quietly that only Becky could hear, "That boy's crazy . . ."

Becky was taking care of her grandfather because two weeks earlier her mother had been diagnosed with lung cancer. She seemed to go from having an annoying cough to dying in about five days! Becky could handle everything but her mother's dying. Her mother wasn't even sixty-years-old. She didn't smoke. It didn't make any sense. Three weeks ago, on Christmas Eve, her mother was reading *The Little Match Girl*, surrounded by fifteen grandchildren. Thirty minutes ago, as Becky watched her lying there, dying on her bed in the sunroom, her mother seemed to be trying to lie perfectly still so she wouldn't choke to death. Becky had the feeling that somehow the fluid was filling her lungs and backing up in her throat, and that if her mother dared move or breathe deeply, that subtle surface tension would break, and she would suffocate. Her mother was showing amazing dignity and courage, but it was just too horrible. It was intolerable. One big gulp of air and her mother would drown.

Becky had always looked young for her age, and this was true at age thirty-five, as well. She was tall, handsome, and powerful-looking, like her granddad. She was lean like her granddad, as well, except, of course, when she was pregnant. Unconsciously, she was standing in the grocery store line massaging Ruby's neck and shoulders; she had guided her grandfather around in front of them now and kept some of her senses tuned on him. Ruby's neck and shoulder muscles were astonishing for a six-year-old, boy or girl, and she guessed they should be with all the hard physical work Ruby had done over the years on her various programs. Becky realized she was staring at a *National Enquirer* with the headline: "World's largest boy—12-year-old weighs 585 lbs., and is *still growing!*" The boy was standing there on the cover, naked except for some kind of canvas-like underwear. He looked every bit of 585 pounds. *Now that would be all I need . . . a 585-pound boy, standing right here in line with Ruby and granddad.* The woman standing right in front of her had a gigantic bag of pork rinds, a big tub of I Can't Believe It's Not Butter, and two two-liter bottles of Mountain Dew. For half a second it seemed funny to Becky that this woman might be taking this home to her 585-pound twelve-year-old.

Then she saw a *Redbook* headline that just about made her jump: "23 Ways to Drive Him Wild in Bed!" She was mad enough right now at her husband Mike to divorce him, so this didn't seem very amusing to her. In fact, it had been in the back of her mind at the grocery store that tonight would be the turning point. She *would* divorce him—it was inevitable. Tonight, she would ask him to move out. He had no business being an hour and a half late when her baby was due any second. Twenty-three ways . . . what would that be, let's see: pull his penis—that's one way . . . suck his penis—that's two ways . . . put your husband in bed with a nineteen-year-old slut of a secretary at the Sheraton on the south side of town—that's three ways . . . That still left twenty ways to please your husband! Why would *Redbook* take on this topic? Who would be next, Martha Stewart?

She could handle Ruby and her granddad at Kroger's, but she shouldn't have to. She was nine months pregnant. Where the hell was Mike when he was supposed to be home? Where the hell was he two hundred other nights of the year! Just at that moment, she felt Ruby's neck tightening up in that old familiar, awful way. Ruby was beginning to have a seizure, and Becky knew there was no stopping it. Becky would have to deal with it *all* in public tonight. As usual, Ruby's shoulders and arms arched up like she was preparing for some kind of dive—like an Olympic swimmer ready to start a race—at the very moment her knees buckled and her jaw clenched and her breathing stopped. It was hard for Becky to hold Ruby because of Becky's huge stomach. *Oh God,* she thought, with some irony but some real panic, *I'm going to strain so much stopping Ruby from falling, I'll start to have this baby!* Ruby was pretty much dead weight now, but Becky had her neatly pinned against the candy rack, for the moment, at least.

Becky's strategy with Ruby in public was to act like whatever she did was just the most normal thing in the world. What will she think of next! A seizure, in the grocery store—what an imagination! This approach worked better when they were walking. She would say, "Ruby, what's so funny? What's so funny, now?!" Or just anything. Ruby was a beautiful little girl, with large beautiful dark eyes and her black hair in a ponytail, the very model of a well dressed little girl in Hannah Anderson tights and dress, Patagonia jacket, and GAP cap, but there is only so much nonchalant faking you can do with a severely brain-injured six-year-old having a seizure in the grocery store line. You can hold her at the shoulders, supporting all of her dead weight. You can say the obvious, "Ruby, you're going to be okay! Just hang on! You're a wonderful girl. It's going to be over. You're going to make it."

And, with fifteen or so Kroger's customers and two checkers straining, bug-eyed to see, of course, she starts to come out of it in about thirty seconds, ecstatic and smiling, squealing in delight, just like Becky knew she would. But the game is up now. Everyone sees the well-dressed brain-injured child squealing and drooling and sort of flapping her hands in glee. Part of Becky is sick about it—some horrible, inexplicable cosmic accident has happened to Ruby, that's a fact, and in some weird way Becky's ashamed of her, like it's somehow her fault. But Becky is proud of Ruby, too, and supportive. Ruby has worked thousands of hard hours to be able to walk into this store so her mother can buy the cold-pressed olive oil Ruby needs for her special diet, and right now, Ruby is as happy as can be—she is high as a kite.

Becky has studied seizures seriously and is convinced that all the medicines they now have to cure seizures mainly numb the already-injured brain even more and bloat the body. Ruby needs to have seizures now and then to shake off some horrible cramped poisoned lack of oxygen or something. Becky wishes she could bottle that feeling Ruby has after a seizure so Ruby could feel that way all day long. Becky says to Ruby, "Now I see what's so funny, Ruby. You're a funny, smart, good girl. Let's buy this olive oil and get your granddad back home. I think he needs a little rest, and you need your supper." She can see the eyes being averted from them, but somehow she and Ruby have survived. The young woman clerk with the back of her head weirdly shaved and a synthetic scarlet-and-burgundy-colored strand of hair curling down in the front of her face is ringing up the special olive oil. Becky's ushering her granddad and Ruby past the check-out stand. They've made it. They're going home.

Becky knows it's cold out, but she feels like a stoked-up Franklin stove. Ruby and her granddad seem to be okay in the cold. For Becky, maneuvering herself into the van, or anywhere else, required a great deal of effort, and very precise synchronization of the movements of her arms and legs and belly. Add to this wrestling fifty pounds of Ruby up into the van and into a car seat while shepherding her granddad, and it all became a monumental feat. But she made it, and she knew she would. She debated among playing the new Natalie Merchant CD and the old Allison Krause CD and the Mozart CD. For the benefit of Ruby and her granddad, she put in the Mozart, and was soon glad she had. She loved Mozart. As a teenager she had played on the piano some of the selections on the "The Best of Mozart" CD. Her fingers worked well, and her mind worked well, but it seemed to her she could never make them work together the way Mozart must have. He seemed to think with his fingers! Her granddad was humming along with Mozart. He had a beautiful voice, so beautiful Becky almost burst into tears, and somehow that got her thinking about divorcing Mike. She would start the ball rolling tonight. She knew that now . . . if she could ever get out of Kroger's parking lot and across the busy traffic on Central Street.

For some reason, thinking about Mike reminded her of the show she'd seen a few days ago on the Discovery Channel about the sexual and mating habits of animals. There were many disturbing parts in the show, especially concerning the troubles of the lioness. First, to keep competing males from their savage fighting, she would mate round the clock with the competing males in turn, on an average of once every twenty minutes for three days, something like three hundred times. Finally, there would be a winner, and the triumphant male would kill the cubs she had by a previous father so that the lioness would stay in heat, and they showed the male doing this—mechanically and cold-bloodedly biting into the necks of each of the cubs in turn. Becky was sickened and outraged; luckily she had rushed her eight-year-old daughter, Claire, out of the room soon after this show started. She encouraged Claire to watch PBS, and the Learning Channel, and the Discovery Channel, but some of the programming on these channels was more disturbing to her than those stupid slime fights among kids on Nickelodeon. It's good to know how things work in the world, but on one of those shows Becky was absolutely astonished to see what had to be the three-foot penis of a male elk arcing up into the female. She was glad Claire missed that!

Last week Becky had watched *Amadeus* with Claire. She was really glad she did, in general—it was just so much fun to sit with Claire and watch her learn things a-mile-a-minute—but, through one scene after another, Becky was wincing and covering Claire's eyes or asking her if she were okay. By the time Mozart's body was thrown in a bag and dumped unceremoniously in a mass grave outside Vienna, Becky had resigned herself to finishing the movie with Claire. Claire was so wide-eyed after this scene that Becky said to her, "Maybe I shouldn't have let you see this movie! Are you okay?" Claire answered, "*I'm* okay, but you wouldn't want to let a *little* kid see this movie!" This seemed like a funny comment from someone barely four feet tall and not quite forty-four pounds.

Traffic was backed up for blocks on Central. Up ahead, at the Taco Bell, Becky saw an uncanny sight. She glanced up at the sign looming over Taco Bell far above the traffic, and it said, "Share Our Shame." Their food was so close to non-food that it actually seemed like a perfect slogan for Taco Bell. On looking closer, as the traffic started moving on Central again, she noticed the sign said, "Try Our Shakes."

Pulling up in her driveway, Becky noticed Mike's cherry-red Grand Cherokee. This was it. She was going to ask him to move out . . . now—tonight. She felt he had serious trouble taking responsibility for his family since Ruby's severe problems surfaced. For the past four years, the problem was especially aggravated. He avoided his family's problems by not facing them. He seemed to come and go as he pleased, whatever family crisis was being played out. She had had it, ironically, on the day her new baby was due. She was going to call the baby Jack, after her granddad . . . despite his behavioral lapse in Kroger's. Sometimes the wiring in his brain seemed to short circuit, but for most of his life he had been a forceful *and* tender-hearted man (sadly, this was truer with her children than his own). With her children, he had always been so careful, and loving, and gentle, and solicitous, even when he threw them up in the air, squealing, and caught them—she had read that was one of the best things you could do for a young child's brain, just don't drop them! And he never did.

She realized she had just been sitting in her driveway, with Ruby slumped forward in her seatbelt sleeping, and her grandad humming what seemed to be "Dixie." She had never heard the "Dixie"-humming side of him before, although he loved old songs like "After the Ball Was Over" and even songs like "Claire de Lune" (in fact, this had been the inspiration for Claire's name). She heaved herself up and out of the van, and opening the door for her grandfather, she said, "Granddad, it's time to rock and roll!"

He responded grumpily, "And way past time, too!" It was hard for her to imagine how life would continue—too many things were breaking down and going dreadfully wrong. Still, it looked like, from now on, pretty much every minute would be wildly interesting.

She wrangled Ruby out of her seatbelt and somehow lifted her out of the van. Together, the three of them, like "The Spirit of Liberty," limped, and huffed, and dragged themselves into the house. It was already six-thirty.

Claire ran up and said, "Mom! I just made a song on the computer using dog notes, then all cat notes! Do you wanna hear it?"

Becky hugged her tight, and kept hugging her; it seemed like neither Becky nor Claire could let go. Claire just kept hugging back, and Becky didn't want to let go of the embrace, either. Claire was the most sensitive and loving child Becky had ever seen. Becky couldn't figure out exactly why; she just was. Becky said, "Claire, I don't want you to worry, but I'm asking your father to move out of the house. I don't know what will happen. . . . I'll listen to the dog and cat song you composed later, okay?"

Claire, in her new role as mother, said, "Don't worry, Mama. I talked to Alice about this—a lot. She wondered—you know, if this might happen soon. Don't worry . . ."

Mike came in on them at that moment, and the sound of a basketball game was shrill in the background, coming through the door he had left open. The announcer was saying, "At this point in the game, a key player just has to step up. It's that simple . . . ."

Mike came up and asked his wife if everything were okay, seeming to light the fuse of a ferocious anger that had been bottled up far too long. Becky answered, "No, Mike, everything is *not* okay. It hasn't been okay in a long, long time. It's after six-thirty! *WHERE WERE YOU!* I could be in labor by now. You said you'd be home right after five!" Becky was holding her stomach, supporting it, somehow trying to protect the baby inside from her anger. "Ruby has to stay on her diet, or you know how she gets! All the hard work she does goes right down the drain! She needs that diet! We were out of that special olive oil; I've waited eight days for fifteen extra minutes to go to the goddamned store! Where the hell were you! Tonight, last night, Friday night? Granddad's here! Claire's here! Ruby's here! Claire's eight years old, Mike, and she's more responsible to her family than you are. Mike, whose family do you think this is?" she asked, angrily sweeping her arm around in a gesture to include Ruby, her granddad, and Claire. Ruby was sort of rocking back and forth; she seemed as tickled as can be (sometimes she really enjoyed seeing people other than her have some real trouble for once). Becky's granddad seemed absolutely ready to strike Mike when the moment called for it. Claire hugged her mom's leg, and Becky saw she was scowling at Mike, with her bottom lip pushed out. It struck Becky that this really had to hurt Mike.

Becky's outburst calmed her down. She stood in the calm wake of her anger and looked at Mike objectively. He still had most of his Robert Redford good looks at thirty-seven, and he was in incredible physical shape. But where did he get that thin tie! Who helped him pick that out! He looked like some executive disco mountain climber. Mike was in the middle of sighing that sigh that men use when women are being hysterical, and they have worked, and worked, and worked for their family. "It's *your* family, Becky . . . it always has been . . . it always has been . . ."

Becky's anger stayed deflated. She couldn't argue if Mike wouldn't, but then Mike continued, "I helped and helped and helped with Ruby. I helped all anyone could . . . ."

Becky answered, calm now, rubbing Claire's back, "I know you did, Mike. You gave it everything you had for a year or two. But Ruby's six now; she still needs your help. We're getting somewhere with her, finally!"

"But I did everything a man could do," Mike said.

"Well, Mike, you did all *you* could do. I think some men would have done better. . . . I want you to move out, Mike. I want you to move out tonight. The people living in this house should be part of this family *now*. I don't know, Mike, maybe you could go stay at that Sheraton over on the south side of town."

"Becky, that was *four years ago*! You never, ever, ever let anything go! You always say I do exactly what I want! That's not true. I almost never do what I want, but *you* do! You do exactly what you want. You always have. You built this life."

Just as Mike won his first point, the war was over. Becky said, "I know, Mike, you tried. You did your best. This *is* my life. I'm not letting *any* of it go. I *did* do what I wanted, but I *didn't* sleep with my teenaged secretary, and I didn't abandon my eight-year-old daughter and my six-year-old brain-injured daughter. I've talked to Jake Evans at Pace, Evans, and Sheer. He says we'll get the house; we'll get by. It wasn't one thing, Mike, it was ten thousand things. You should leave—leave now!" And then she said the weirdest thing, that show about the lioness in the back of her mind, "You should be defending our family, not using your brute strength to kill the helpless." She knew she was so mad she was being irrational, and that what she said wouldn't make any sense to Mike, but it felt *great* as she was saying it.

Mike shocked everyone. He swung at the antique lamp standing by the sofa and sent it sailing along the slick wooden floor, with light bulbs shattering. He seemed to be to the door and headed out before the lamp stopped skidding about fifteen feet from where it had stood.

Becky's granddad startled everyone who was left by exclaiming vigorously, shaking his fist after the retreating Mike, "*I'll* rip your fucking head off if you mess with *my* girl again! I'll kill you quick!"

Her mother's dying had kept Becky's mind swirling with thoughts about immortality. However, the moment Becky walked into her mother's house that Tuesday night with Claire and her granddad—two nights after she had asked Mike to leave—all such abstract thoughts vanished from Becky's mind. Her mother was clinging to this life by a thread, and Becky focused completely on that.

Much of the mystery about the cause of her mother's cancer had been straightened out, for Becky, at least, late the night before when Becky had been sitting alone with her mother. Her mother could only speak in the faintest, agonizing whispers, but it had been important for Helen to tell this to Becky. Helen told her, painful bit by painful bit, that when she was an infant, back when they really didn't know much about X-rays, her mother had had a powerful X-ray done on Helen every week for many months. Either Helen had swallowed something, or her mother feared she *might have* swallowed something—Becky never got this point straight. In any case, when the news began to come out about how harmful X-rays could be, Helen's mother told her that she would die young. This last part seemed to be the clincher. Helen *was* dying young.

Becky grabbed on to that explanation—not that *any* explanation would help. It made a certain kind of weird sense; there certainly seemed to be no other cause. Becky related, in a way. Claire had swallowed a large round pink barrette when she was about eighteen months old. Claire's older cousins had been playing with her earlier, teaching her how to chew gum, and, later, she was playing an imaginary game of "chewing gum" when it happened. Becky had gone into orbit with worry. Claire wasn't choking, so she didn't rush her to the emergency room, but she saw the doctor and read everything she could on the subject.

She became convinced, soon, that if the child didn't choke when some object was swallowed, they would probably be okay. In fact, in one of the books about handling medical emergencies for children, the author told the story of his friend in medical school breaking up a drinking glass and swallowing the pieces every Friday afternoon. The med student charged two dollars apiece for people to see this exhibition, and he used the money to go drinking over the weekend. The point being: parents, don't panic if your child swallows something. If they don't choke, and it isn't poison, they'll probably be okay—the stomach has a way of dealing with most foreign objects. Claire's barrette came out two weeks after she swallowed it. It had never hurt her going in, and it didn't hurt her coming out. Claire was fine. The horrible irony in what happened to Becky's mother, though, is that the parental anxiety on her mother's part seemed to be costing Helen her life now. She hadn't been in danger when she was an infant, but, because of the X-rays, now she *was* choking to death.

Two weeks before (it seemed like months and months), all the doctors decided Helen was dying and there really wasn't much to be done about it at this point—except to make her comfortable through Hospice. All the family had finally agreed, after about two days of fevered planning and checking this or that last possibility, to let her die peacefully, if that were possible. A day or so later, Helen said, almost comically, "Well, what's next? What do we do now?" It seemed so odd. She was dying, but she didn't feel very bad. It was certain she would die, but she didn't feel very sick. Intense and lasting pain had finally sent Helen to the doctor in the first place, but, ironically, when it was all decided that nothing could be done, there was a kind of lull in the pain.

No one had an answer for Helen about what was to be done next, other than to shower love on her every possible minute, and yet to try to let her rest when she started feeling bad physically again in a few days. Her spirits stayed very positive, considering. She showed great dignity and courage throughout, and within a day or two she seemed plenty sick enough to die, and to die at any minute. Everyone who saw her wondered how she could be so calm as she faced choking every minute. They all wondered if they could hold out in that situation hour after hour, day after day, and they all knew they couldn't possibly do it. It just wasn't something humans beings could do.

For the last ten days or so, Becky and her sisters had taken their turns staying with Helen. Becky checked on her mother every morning and afternoon and night, but her official time slot was from midnight until three in the morning. Helen had always been an especially strong woman, and it was hard for Becky to see her so weak and scared and dependent, and it was simply impossible for her to come to terms with her mother's dying.

It had surprised her how well some of the younger kids, eleven or twelve, were doing with their turns caring for their grandmother. They had only very short sessions every few days, but they were careful, watchful, compassionate, and efficient in their care of their grandmother. It broke her heart, but made her proud, as well, to see her nieces and nephews delicately give their grandmother a wet sponge so she could get a few drops of water into her system. This was an especially troubling procedure because she stayed desperately thirsty, yet couldn't really swallow, and seemed always on the verge of drowning from the inside.

They read to her and wiped her forehead with a cool washcloth. One nephew, Ben, was reading *The Secret Garden*, always one of Helen's favorites, and one niece, Jenny, was reading *My Darling, My Hamburger*, or some book like that. That didn't seem like an especially appropriate choice, but Helen seemed agreeable. At first, Becky wondered if Claire should keep her grandmother company as she died. Becky was worried that that might traumatize an eight-year-old, but, when she thought about it, the only people she knew who had been especially traumatized by a "natural" death were those children completely kept in the dark about what was happening.

It seemed very natural for Claire to stay with her grandmother. As a matter of fact, Claire actually seemed more comfortable than the older kids, and she rattled on and on about dreams she'd had recently and things like that. It was usually quite touching, but she had walked in on Claire and Helen alone late the afternoon before and Claire was telling Helen about a terrible dream she had, "See, they had this show in St. Louis, where everyone had to fix their hair as neat as they could in five minutes, and this one woman had matches all in her hair and started a fire, and the fire went everywhere. She tried to push me in, but I jumped out." Becky quickly veered her daughter onto another topic, but what impressed her the most was the way Claire was gently holding Helen's hand and stroking it. Helen seemed as relaxed and comfortable as Becky had seen her since all this started.

That Wednesday night, Becky's sisters and brothers were all gathered around, and it was a very hushed scene. They were more and more convinced their mother would die any minute. They had never seen her so scared, and it seemed like she might choke at any minute. The Hospice nurses hadn't set up any suction devices, because Helen hadn't wanted such intervention, but they had left morphine for the pain. Helen had steadily refused to take any right along. This night, a very strong majority of her children present favored giving her mother morphine, and so did her father, David, although this whole ordeal seemed to have left him unsure about anything. He seemed completely helpless. As usual, Becky was the family spokesperson. She said, "Mama, we've all talked about it—Daddy and Robert and John and Virginia and Alice [she only listed the pro morphine votes]—and we think it's time for you to take something strong for pain."

Her mother seemed to be listening. That horrible liquid sound as she breathed so carefully was unbearable, though.

"Mama, the Hospice nurse said to put this morphine tablet right under your tongue. I think you should do it, Mama. It might help you. They gave you this medicine for a reason."

To that, her mother gave the slightest affirmative nod. Becky glanced around the room. Others had seen it, too. Becky got out the small morphine pill, surprised at how small and soft and chalky it was. There was no pharmaceutical symbol on it; it seemed almost crudely handmade. Becky carefully put the pill under her mother's tongue. Despite that awful wet sound, her mother's lips—and Becky knew this very well already—were dry, and even the inside of her mouth seemed dry and papery, easy to bruise.

Becky and those assembled were prepared for Helen to go into a deep sleep, one from which she would never wake up. There was sort of a giant, sad embrace by the twenty or so people in the room, adults and children. People cried quietly, held each other's hands, hugged, and looked down, not speaking, and not looking at anything in specific.

Becky noted that she had given her mother the morphine at eight-twenty, according to the old clock on her mother's bedside table. When Helen's eyes popped wide open, Becky noticed it was 8:27. There was a wry and calm smile on Helen's face. She said very softly, but very distinctly, "You know, I could get used to this!"

The mood in the room went soaring. Suddenly, it seemed like Helen could breathe, and all the talk about her dying seemed to be some weird miscalculation. She wasn't scared anymore. There was no wet sound in her throat. She could breathe again. People started to whisper to each other, "She's not afraid anymore."

Becky hugged her mother very tenderly and very carefully. Everyone had been treating her throat and chest as if it were the thinnest eggshell that had already been cracked, and, of course, Becky's being pregnant hadn't been helping her maneuver carefully around her mother.

For about thirty minutes, Becky's mother was the life of the party. She didn't even slur her words very much. She said things like, "This is great . . . ! You could just sit out in the back yard on a summer day and take this and drink iced tea . . . or beer [which was very funny to everyone because Helen hadn't had a beer in twenty years] . . . watch the stars come out . . . listen to the breeze in the trees. You know, Virginia sang that hymn to me over the phone today, something about 'Ready to Go, Ready to Stay.' You know, I wasn't ready to go *or* ready to stay! I just couldn't get comfortable. I couldn't breathe. I kept feeling like I was going to choke. Why didn't I take this earlier!"

About that time, Becky's grandfather came up to Helen, and started talking. He seemed to have found about six weeks' worth of lucidity all at once. "Honey, you were always the best girl . . . I want you to know. You helped your mama and me all your life. You seemed to be everybody's mama all along, even when you were just a little girl. You helped us all make it, and now. . ."When his voice trailed off, everyone in the room was crying softly.

Helen held up her hand a fraction of a inch to touch her father's hand. Somehow, she just couldn't lift it up to him. She said, "I know, Daddy. You will all help each other now, don't worry. I love you, Daddy. You help Becky, now, okay?"

It was a pitch black night outside the sunroom windows, but there was a peaceful glow of happiness as long as Helen stayed awake and happy. When she drifted off to sleep in about thirty minutes, there was definitely a new kind of peace and optimism in the room.

Thursday afternoon about three-thirty, Becky was coming back to see her mother for the third time since the night before. Her mother was sleeping a great deal more than she had before, but hadn't taken any morphine since the night before. Some were encouraged she was sleeping so much, and some were worried. Becky knew Claire was in with her grandmother, and that comforted her. Becky was leading Ruby into the living room when she heard a faint gasp for air in the sunroom. It was an eerie sound, and it made Becky sort of weak in the knees. She heard Virginia say in faint disbelief, "She's gone, Alice. . ."The scream that everyone in the house heard next from Becky seemed like the most natural thing in the world, "MA-MA!"The kids playing in the basement heard it. The teenagers on the second floor heard it. Her sisters in the kitchen heard it as clearly as if it had come from their own lips. Becky herself did not even realize she had screamed, and she had screamed with all her might, and more. This cry of anguish came from so deep inside her it started long before she was born, and echoed long after her own death. There could be no sound before that sound, and no sound after it. This was entirely appropriate, because that's exactly how deeply Becky loved her mother.

The funeral was on Saturday morning. The day was bright and bitterly cold, with a sheen of ice on everything. Becky had been feeling occasional sharp pains since the middle of the night, and that kind of certain tug and pull, and she knew it was starting. She dressed for the funeral, but, by nine o'clock, when the family was heading to the church for the funeral, Virginia was taking Becky to the hospital. The ice on the driveway and everywhere else worried Becky a great deal. She worried about the baby inside her, and Ruby, and her granddad. She had worked out the care of Ruby and her granddad in meticulous detail, and just decided to relax about that. She was locked into something new, and she was ready for it.

It had struck everyone as a perfect day for the funeral, oddly enough. Helen had loved the cold and snow. Well, she loved every kind of weather, but no one knew of anyone who loved the cold and snow like Helen. The sun glinting on the ice seemed to everyone like Helen beaming down from above. It just seemed to everyone that she had arranged all this, and was kind of smiling, and happy, and laughing about it. Of course, Becky was worried about that long, awful, slick drive way out in the country to the cemetery after the service in town. She didn't see how anyone could stand outside for long in that bitter cold.

When Becky got to the hospital, the contractions were already coming every five minutes. The pain and the situation distracted her some, but she missed her mother desperately. She had never done anything important without her mother's being there. She wasn't so much sad for herself—she could feel that her mother was a part of her, now more than ever—she was sad for her mother. Her mother had reached a point in life when she could enjoy life, almost all day, every day. It was intolerable to think of that joy ripped away from her mom. On the other hand, it made Becky chuckle to think of her mom fighting all the doctors and nurses at the hospital for her daughter's rights during this birth. She had done this when Ruby had been born; she had done it with every one of her grandchildren born in a hospital. Maybe the doctor didn't feel like coming in at three in the morning, whatever it was. Helen was willing to set them all straight in a hurry. There was nothing more important on this earth than her children and grandchildren. The whole hospital was always in an uproar in an hour's time. Becky felt she could get a better result from the nurses and doctors simply being nice to them, and giving them a little dignity. They were just doing what they had to do. They weren't going to switch to natural and reasonable childbirth methods the minute Becky Hawkins arrived in the hospital!

Becky had fantasized a quick and easy delivery. Six hours of labor later, she seemed in an endless and deadly wrestling match with pain and pressure. The birth of Claire had been done with a midwife and had been quick, intense, and natural. In a hospital, they seemed intentionally to do almost everything against the grain. About four that afternoon, Becky gave in and took an epidural shot to ease the pain. She knew this would slow the birth even a little longer, but she didn't care at this point. She had been through enough the last few days.

Nine hours after she had entered the hospital, the baby heaved out from inside her in a wet rush into the world. The doctor had used the forceps a little, and the idea of that giant metal shoehorn prying against her baby's soft head gave her an awful, queasy feeling, even in the midst of that last incredible wave of pain that the baby arrived into the world on. It was clear to Becky and her sister Alice and everyone on the medical team how vital and healthy this baby was. Of course, Ruby's problem—whatever it was, exactly, and whatever caused it—had been on her mind for much of this past nine months.

She had already told everyone who worked with her in the maternity suite, or whatever they called it, that her baby's name was Jack. He was named for his granddad, but she had always loved that name since coming upon "good old bulldog Jack" in *Little House in the Big Woods*. Her red, red baby was slippery and strong and tense and active. The second the nurses took him from her arms and lay him on the super-heated lighted tray next to her bed, he started to squirt a surprising stream of urine straight up into the air. Becky was still a little woozy from the epidural, and she surprised the nurses by saying, "They're born squirting, and they die squirting." She didn't know exactly what she meant, but it made her think of that ridiculous dream she had had once with men having some weird *Wide World of Sports*-type semen-squirting contest. It was a ridiculous and awful dream, with men squirting from horseback, and from motorcycles, and pole vaulting, and doing back flips—men squirting extravagantly everywhere, with the result that soon the arena looked like the way they foam an airport runway preparing for a crash. Of course, Jack seemed simply innocent and healthy in his exuberant squirting.

It was clear her baby knew her, right from the first, and, at one point early on, he looked right at her. He was so healthy and strong. But, soon, the medical establishment had subdued him. They poked a needle into his thigh. They dried him off and powdered him, and, incredibly, they took him away from her. She was ready to fight that, but, before she knew it, she was waking up—the windows showed nothing but the dark night now—and they had brought him back.

The nurse was telling Becky that her . . . husband? . . . had been by. Her ex-husband? Becky didn't bite, refusing to get into explaining the situation. "Good-looking guy . . ." the nurse said softly, half to Becky and half to herself as she turned away. In a funny way, Becky was glad Mike came by. He was a good part-time parent. That was fine with her. She would even encourage that, but his days of having the luxury of pretending to be a full-time parent were over. She would never again accept as a tolerable definition of a good man that "he could be worse"! Now she was wrapped up in her baby. She was wildly in love with this baby, and Jack seemed to sense that in her cooing talk. For all Becky knew, he was thinking, "Good! She's okay. She's healthy! She's perfect!"

Becky knew she couldn't really begin nursing yet—she knew from much experience exactly how long it would take the milk to come in—and she knew it would be a hardship getting started and working through things like painfully cracked nipples early on. But she held her child up to her breast, and he took the nipple almost instantly. She knew that little bit of colostrum was unbelievably powerful medicine for a newborn. The way he tugged gently and pulled strongly in an eager cycle somehow reached a different level of her being, one long submerged, but one she recognized immediately. She was intimately familiar with it. That gentle, but somehow voracious, tugging rooted her firmly and comfortably in this world. It was a fulfilling and full world in which she belonged.

When her baby's gums slipped off her nipple with kind of a pop, she got kind of a new perspective on things. Things had been happening so fast, so overwhelmingly. She took an instant to take the long view, her baby hugged to her breast. Looking at the chaos of our exploding universe, human life was an absolute miracle—from any way you choose to look at it. Everything had to be totally right to create and sustain it. A million, million variables had to align with exquisite precision for this perfection to happen—the tilt and rotation of the earth had to be just so, the distance from the sun, the pull of the moon, and all the elaborately interconnected orbits. . . . Given this, *anything* seemed possible. Still, she also knew, as she felt the heat and spirit from her baby (with his heart beating so strongly against her), and felt him begin to nurse again with renewed urgency, that this was her truest immortality.

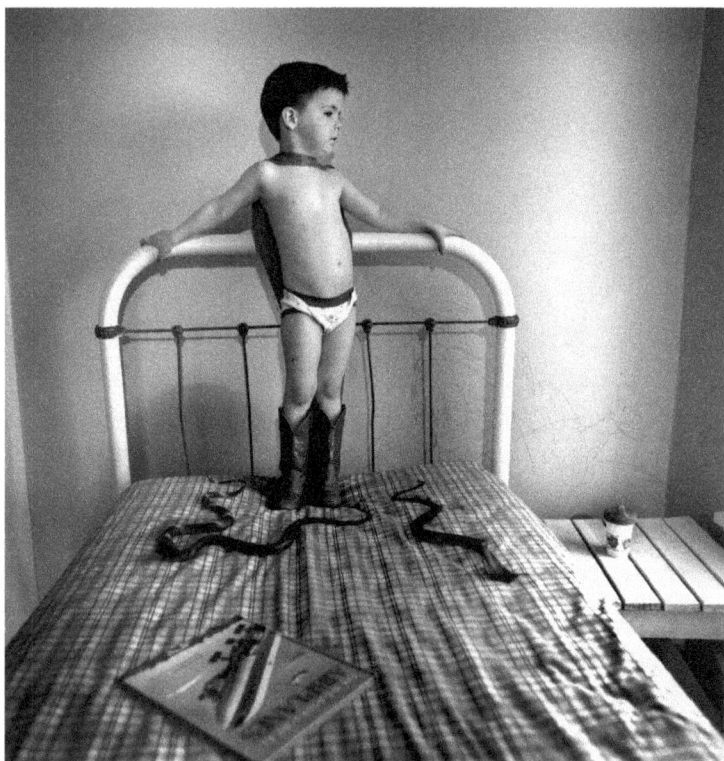

TESTOSTERONE

As Claire came up to the "on-deck circle," getting ready to bat for the first time in a ten-and-under softball league game, Becky felt like one of the seven Flying Wallendas balancing on the high-wire. Twenty minutes before, the babysitter for Becky's other daughter, Ruby, now eight, had canceled unexpectedly with no notice whatsoever. Ruby was robustly rocking back and forth next to Becky, smiling hugely and flapping her hands in glee. Despite her beauty, her severe brain injury was usually quickly apparent, and Becky was hesitant to subject her to many public situations. Part of Becky's precarious balance on the high wire was that, in one part of her mind, she knew she would be inconsolable if she stopped and analyzed how others saw Ruby, so she didn't stop in that part of her mind. Her daughter was happy now, and that was a wonderful thing in itself—that was easily the most important thing, she realized. Amidst the general hubbub of the softball game, she hugged her daughter close and said to her, "You're a wonderful girl, Ruby—a big, smart, wonderful girl. I'm glad you're having fun. I love you *so* much!" This caused Ruby to flap her hands even more vigorously and squeal so exuberantly she seemed ready to take flight.

Becky's two-year-old son, Jack, had already climbed up a couple of feet on a pipe support on the batter's cage next to where her eighty-eight-year-old grandfather was standing. These two had been macho peas in a pod lately and seemed right in their element at the game. Budding dementia unleashed streams of colorful and derogatory language from her always aggressive granddad, who was yelling at the second baseman up to bat for Claire's team, "Hit the cob-bam doll! Just hit the bam doll!"

His alter-ego, Jack, jumped right in behind him, yelling, "Dan! Ball! Dan ball, now!" If her grandfather's pronunciation were just a touch clearer, he would have already been in a brawl with the parents of the opposing Rugrats' team. He had developed quite a mouth for being such a religious zealot in the past. To top it off, Becky's ex-husband, Mike, was coaching at first base. It aggravated Becky how sensitive he was with these girls, how obviously good a coach he was. He was yelling at the batter from his first base coach's box, "Grip it and rip it, Nicole!" Nicole seemed to have about one chance in a thousand of actually making contact with the ball, let alone "ripping it," but his spunky and encouraging comments took just the right tone and seemed to focus both her will and her bat as she whacked the ball lobbed to her skidding foul down the first-base line.

As Becky tried to focus in on the game, she noticed that the theme song from that weird cartoon Claire, Jack, and her granddad had been watching lately on Nickelodeon, "SpongeBob SquarePants," was running through her mind: "Who lives in a pineapple under the sea . . . ?: SpongeBob! SquarePants! . . ." Nicole's mother, Tracy, sitting next to Becky, was looking across at Ruby with curiosity and tenderness. Somehow, that lulled Becky with a warm and comforting feeling. The spiderweb of worries she had projected out toward Claire and Jack and her granddad and Ruby seemed for the moment more like a safety net, especially with Ruby being so happy and many of her sisters and friends around her on the bleachers. Tracy called out to her daughter as she swung at a ball a good three yards out of her reach, "Good effort, Nicole! Way to swing! You can do it!"

Becky winced as her granddad piped up with something that sounded to her like, "Holy Shit on the Roof!"

She called out to him reflexively, "Granddad! . . . Granddad, sweetie, why don't you take Jack to get some lemonade or something? Come over here, honey. . ."

 He scooped up Jack and headed over to her on the bleachers, where he took the two one-dollar bills she held up. "Sure thing," he said with a cocky laugh, "that's about the only way *I'm* gonna score tonight!" His fierce love for Jack seemed palpable in the way he held the boy in his arms and wrestled around with him and the way the two joked and talked and bubbled and cooed and hugged. As they headed for the concession stand, she dreaded to think what trouble they could get into. It was a desperate move to let them go alone—normally, she wouldn't dream of leaving them on their own under any circumstances—but she didn't really see any choice. The time limit on these games was one hour—she was cold-bloodedly determined to make it!

Nicole had struck out and had to scamper back to pick up her bat as Claire was walking up to the plate. Becky was bathed in encouraging comments about her daughter's cute shoes, shorts, and haircut, while the helpful chorus of advice ("Just meet the ball with the bat!" "You can do it, Claire!") echoed around Becky and out to Claire. Claire had a wide-eyed, terrified look walking to the plate, but once she got there, she pounded the plate with the bat, something Mike must have taught her. He had been working with Claire lately in a thoughtful, cheerful, consistent way that made Becky look at her ex-husband in a new light for a moment. Doug Johnson, Claire's coach, was lobbing the ball over the plate pretty well, but Claire missed badly on two swings and let two good pitches go without swinging. The girls got a maximum of five pitches, so the entire Cosmic Comets' rooting section was emphasizing to Claire to swing at the next pitch, no matter what, and she nicked the ball just enough that it trickled out in front of her about three feet. Claire stood there for a second or two while Comets fans screamed in agony, "Run, Claire, run! Run to first base! Fair ball! Run!" Finally, Claire did run (as the Rugrats' parents took their turn yelling desperately, "Lucy, throw the ball! Throw the ball to first!"), and Becky was amazed how quickly Claire raced to first base once she got going. Claire and Mike were hugging and high-fiving like crazy on first base. It was a remarkable moment. Claire was so delighted her ponytail seemed to be caught in a hurricane as it whipped wildly around. The Comets had their first base hit of the season, and Mike was a perfect mirror of his daughter's satisfaction. When the pandemonium died down a little, Tracy nudged Becky and said wistfully, "Mike is just such a beautiful man. I keep looking at him, and I just can't get over how good looking he is—just the way he looks in those shorts . . . I mean he's always been good looking, but he just seems so happy out there with Claire."

"Looking good has never been Mike's problem," Becky said bitterly. She hated the meanness and pettiness in her voice, but only because Nicole didn't understand—she hadn't really known Mike and her before. Mike had earned the way she felt about him, and dozens and dozens of times worse, but all Becky said to Tracy was, "Mike's done a good job practicing with Claire the last couple of weeks. . . ."

What was really on her mind, though, was how she had been noticing lately that Jack reminded her of Mike. Jack, like Mike, just seemed brimful of energy and willfulness, like some kind of muscle-packed testosterone bomb, ready to explode at any moment. Jack was a lot more cuddly than Mike, but he took on everything in his environment in the same physical way, climbing up and jumping off, and whacking and hitting and throwing and pushing and yelling. He was a smart boy, and often tender, but he was just so happy and alive manhandling everything around him. She had continued to nurse him late, like she did with Claire and Ruby, until well after he was one, but it was like nursing a little Sumo wrestler. He worked her over. Sunday morning, he had slipped away after his bath before she had gotten his diaper on him while she ran to answer the phone. When Becky caught up to him, he was walking around upstairs pulling his penis a remarkable distance out in front of him, saying proudly, "Pull! Pull!" She said, "That's good saying 'pull,' but you better hold off on doing things like that in public! That's good saying 'pull,' though, really good." Earlier last week she was changing his diaper when he said, "Snake! Big snake in dere! Snake!" This was obviously a snake he wasn't afraid of. Lately, he had been pointing out snakes and monsters everywhere, so maybe she was jumping to conclusions. Becky just generally felt better keeping his diaper on; that seemed to be the safest thing. To top it off, Claire and Becky's youngest sister, Jenny, had taught him to say that the models in fashion magazines were "hot." The funny thing, though, was he seemed to have absolutely grown-up tastes concerning women. It just seemed eerie how much like Mike he was, but she knew Jack was perfectly innocent. Did that make Mike innocent, as well . . . no, she hadn't gotten to that point yet. One obvious difference was that Jack was two years old, and Mike almost forty. Another was that Jack, when he was nursing, had never gone around chasing other mothers and nursing with them!

Becky had lost the thread of the softball game in front of her. Claire had been stranded on second base when the inning was over, but didn't seem to mind. The Rugrats were in the middle of batting. A big red-headed girl with "Lefty" written on the back of her navy blue jersey swaggered up to bat. Becky's sister Jordan whispered down to Nicole and her, "That girl looks about fourteen! I hope she doesn't plow into Stacy!" The opposing bleachers were only separated by about ten feet, so the parents and grandparents faced the challenge of being fiercely partisan and loudly supportive and yet not overtly offensive to the opposition. Lefty whacked the ball with great power toward the gap between first and second. She was lounging on first base long before the ball was relayed to Claire at first. Claire didn't catch the ball thrown at her face, but she knocked it down and picked it up very smartly, menacingly holding the runner on first. Her play was seen as quite a triumph, and there was rejoicing by both teams and their fans. Mike, who stretched his first-base coaching to include defense, patted Claire enthusiastically on the back, and even gallantly congratulated Lefty, seeming to give both girls pointers about what options to consider when the next batter came up to hit.

Ruby was peacefully sucking her thumb with her head in Becky's lap. What panicked Becky now was what had happened to Jack and her granddad. Her worst fear was dealing with a round of poop in public from Ruby or Jack, or, lately, even her granddad. Of course, Ruby and her granddad were simply too big to deal with this way in public. Her greatest fear was that she would have to deal with two of them having this problem at the same time, or all three. This seemed like the ultimate public poop nightmare of all time! To up the ante a little more, Ruby could have one of her seizures (this actually didn't seem that unlikely, in fact)—Becky could handle that, if it was *just* that. Of course, the ultimate cherry on top would be her granddad having a stroke . . . or assaulting somebody. He was a strong old man, and very quick to react to an insult or threat, real or imagined. He was like a Rottweiler with her kids, perfectly gentle and mild, but strangers better watch out. That thought got her shifting Ruby's head over to Tracy's lap, asking Tracy's help with whispers and gestures, and sneaking away as discreetly as she could, but finding herself almost in a trot after the first few steps, in search of Jack and her granddad.

There were about ten softball fields radiating out from a concession stand in the center at the Merritt Park Softball Complex. Becky scurried by the neighboring fields, scanning for Jack and her granddad. Before long, she was running toward the concession stand. As she neared the windows where customers bought slurpees and hot dogs and ice cream, she panicked because she couldn't see Jack or her granddad, then she spotted her granddad, all six-foot-one of him, standing by a picnic table on the far side of the concession stand, but something didn't make sense. . . . She didn't see Jack! That weird kind of electric shock hit her at that point. That awful doomed realization of what it was like to lose a child. She calmly, desperately, hopelessly saw it all in that moment. This is what it felt like to lose a child. It would never get any better than this—he was gone! How could she have let it happen! That feeling of shock just kept radiating out from her and into her. She kept running toward her granddad, scanning the area around him and behind him. Then, back behind the steel beam jutting out to support the back side of the roof of the concession stand, she spotted a red swatch of a shirt like Jack had on, then she spotted Jack, feeding a little pug-nosed black and white Chinese dog a chocolate ice cream cone. She realized she was breathless and panting like she had run a long race as fast as she could . . . she just couldn't catch her breath.

She lifted him up to hug him tightly, but even in her relief she tried to keep his hand with the dripping ice cream away from her top. When he was first jerked up, he exclaimed, "Hey!" in that way that seemed so cute and grown up to Becky, but when he saw it was her, he said, "Ma-ma!" in that loving, lingering way he had, "Ma-ma!"

Off to the side, Becky noticed that her granddad was talking to a pretty teenaged girl with a bare midriff, and that while he was being his old charming self to the girl, he seemed to have a very menacing attitude toward a little six-year-old boy next to them. Becky figured that trouble was brewing whichever way this went (he had a very cruel streak towards males in general, except for her son, Jack), but she needed to get Jack, who looked like his face had been hit with a chocolate ice cream bomb, straightened away.

She started in with Jack, but kept one eye and ear on her granddad. She said, "Jack, what happened to *you*!"

He answered enthusiastically, "I have ice cream, Mama, *ice cream*!"

She said, "I see that. You *do* have ice cream, and that little dog has ice cream, and there's ice cream all over your face!"

He answered analytically, "Dog eat ice cream all up!"

Now she was tuning in on her grandfather's conversation as it seemed to turn more desperate. He was saying, "You see that little boy over there. He's the cob-damdest ball player you ever seen. He could throw a ball overhand when he was six months old! I tell you he throws the ball hard! Just give him a ball; he's a doll-damb Dizzy Dean, and he's just two years old!" Becky noticed that the teenager trapped by her granddad had a ring in her navel—that kind of thing always gave Becky the willies; the teenager seemed to think her granddad was quite a character, but she seemed a little nervous, too. ". . . his daddy's no damned good . . . he's a good ball player, but, otherwise, he's just not worth a monkey's be-hind . . ." Then a truly ominous look flickered across her granddad's face, "But, you know, I think that little boy there has plumb stolen my chocolate ice cream! Here I'm talkin' to you, and that little monkey wrench . . ."

By that point Becky had already shoved Jack in her granddad's arms and was guiding him away from the miniature Britney Spears and her brother at a pretty rapid clip, with the general goal of getting Jack to a bathroom to clean him up. Realizing her granddad couldn't go in the women's restroom, she veered off towards a water fountain. As she was holding Jack horizontal and washing his face with her hand, the ice cream, of course, plopped out of the cone he was holding, and he screamed like he'd been stabbed. Becky, sort of wedging her grandfather against the bathroom wall with her leg, assured Jack, "You'll be okay . . . you'll be just fine. Eating a big load of sugar isn't a great idea at any time, and sharing your ice cream with a dog is not a great idea, either. Just relax . . . you'll be just fine! You need to help your mom now! I really need your help now, Jack!" He kept up his wailing just a little too long as she carried him and shepherded her granddad back to Claire's game, and she gave Jack that kind of shake so that he knew she was just about to lose control completely. The rough turbulence of his flight, in that one instant, seemed to calm him considerably, with the only aftermath being his somber hiccupping and his tear-stained face. He had marshaled all his resources into stopping crying. He said, the very picture of the pitiful, "I happy now . . ." then hiccupped. "I happy now, Mama."

Becky was impressed at, and appreciative of, his effort. She hugged his smooth cheek against hers tightly and said, "You're the biggest boy now! You're such a good help to your mom. I love you so much!" They both couldn't stop hugging each other. They just keep desperately hugging and hugging each other.

Her granddad, not wanting to be left out of this family scene, patted them both gently on the back, and said softly to himself, "Yeah, well, it was *my* ice cream. . . . It's easy enough to flush *my* barn doll ice cream down the cob-bam dumper! "

But when he shifted around to look Becky in the eye, he said simply and sincerely, "I love ya, baby . . ." And he gave both of them a gentle hug.

Becky noticed Claire was in the Comets' dugout over on the left side on the field when she positioned Jack and her granddad back against the far side of the batter's cage on that side of the field. She warned them, "Jack, Granddad, the ball can smash your fingers if you keep them inside the fence like that!" Their fingers curled around the sturdy wire mesh, not that she had the time or energy to get them to move their hands. She noticed that the scoreboard behind the outfield fence read Comets 9, Rugrats 11. The numbers were formed by little professional-looking bulbs of light that showed up very well in the increasing dusk. Becky could hear Ruby moaning distractedly back where Tracy was struggling to hold her on the bottom row of the bleachers. She quickly took over for Tracy, saying in sort of a stage whisper, so Tracy could hear but not everyone else, "I'm so sorry . . . was it hard? I couldn't find them at first . . . then Jack was—"

Tracy jumped in saying, "No, no, she was fine, just fine, until a minute ago. . . . Not a problem! Ruby and I did just fine, didn't we, Ruby!" Ruby's response was to jerk her arms and head angrily, kind of thrashing around and groaning and audibly grinding her teeth (a sound that distressed her mother in too many ways to quantify). Some tremendous commotion was going on out on the field at the moment, and Becky didn't even try to understand it all. She just hugged her daughter and rocked the big girl back and forth reassuringly, in the calm center of all the surrounding furor, saying, "Ruby, it's over now . . . you're going to be just fine . . . we're going home any minute." She wondered if Dizzy Dean—whoever *he* was—could have been such a hot ball player if he had to look after kids. "You know," she said to Ruby, "Jack and your granddad can be the biggest brats; you don't need to join them." Ruby kind of perked up at that, paying close attention, and then there was that little laugh of hers. Becky loved that laugh. As usual, Ruby really liked to see others have some serious and embarrassing problems. She really got a kick out of it. Her mom rocked her back and forth, playfully now, saying, "Well, Ruby, I'm glad to see you're happy now! Now let's see what Claire and her team are doing. Can you believe it, I've missed most of the game!"

Tracy was on her feet, chanting with the rest of the Comets' cheering section, "Aim-ee! Aim-ee! Aim-ee!" Becky found herself in an ocean of foot stomping, clapping, and cheering. It seemed like a great happening. She had never imagined softball to be like this. She thought it would be more like stock car racing, or something alien like that, but here were all her friends and family having a whale of a time! When things calmed down and Tracy sat back down, Becky asked her for an update, and Tracy raced into catching her up, saying, "You won't believe it, but we were ahead the whole game until now. Lindsey and Erin have really been hitting the ball, and Claire is so fast, they can hardly get her out. . . . She stops the ball at first base every time; she's doing great. . . . Nicole is hanging in there—at least she hit some foul balls—she feels good about herself. . . . The funniest thing, April just sat down out there at short stop, just sat down and rested in the middle of the inning! That big girl on their team has just been pounding it. She's done most of the damage. She hit it all the way over second base once! Here's Claire again. . . ." With that, she whistled shrilly using two fingers (Becky was always amazed at this maneuver) and stood up yelling, "You can do it, Claire! Stand in there, girl! Just whack it!"

Becky was impressed with the vociferous goodwill and encouragement her daughter was generating. It didn't come naturally to her, but she yelled, "Come on, Claire! You can do it!" Claire glanced back to her and smiled weakly. She was really nervous, it was clear to Becky, and that huge batting helmet seemed to dwarf her. Claire was swinging at the ball well, though, getting so close. On the fourth pitch, she hit a foul zinging outside the third base line. She ran so fast toward first base, she was nearly there before she realized it had gone foul. Her teammates were cheerfully and loudly calling out in unison, "Come on, Claire, you can do it! Put a little power to it!" These girls had a neat rhythm to their cheering, and Becky could already sense that these cheers would get more elaborate and choreographed as the season went along. Claire struck out on the next pitch, but she *had* put a little power to it. She swung hard, she got close to the ball, and it was all very exciting. Becky soon noticed it was a great supportive atmosphere at the game, something she never really expected. The girls and their fans had such a generally great attitude, so supportive, although it was clear both teams and their fans desperately wanted to win. One side groaned miserably and the other cheered wildly at each strike out, or when the ball was thrown ten feet over the first baseman's head. Becky also noticed how physical the game forced these girls to be. Whatever perky attitude you might have, you had to hit the ball, you had to run, you had to throw the ball, and you had to catch the ball or knock it down. Becky didn't know why this all struck her so much as a revelation. She wished she had had a chance to be on a team like this when she was a girl. Partly she could have the luxury of such thoughts because she had placed Jack and her granddad on the far left hand edge of the batter's cage, as far away from the crowd as she could get them, and, so far, they had stayed put. Also, Ruby, was back resting her head peacefully in Becky's lap, sucking her thumb.

Becky's seven-year-old niece, Justine, approached the plate now with a lost look, seeming very frail. Her new short haircut was getting rave reviews from the moms, though, and she was getting a steady stream of encouragement coaching from her coach, Doug, who seemed ready to talk her through this like Ground Control in Houston calmly talked the astronauts through impossible problems. His soothing mantra continued, ". . . just watch the ball . . . just meet the ball with the bat . . . here it comes. . . That's okay, Justine—good swing!" Becky loved this game. Everybody was so supportive, so positive. It was okay to try and fail; in fact, that was a great cause for celebration. As she looked down at Ruby's long, beautiful black eyelashes, and gently massaged her neck and shoulders and scalp, she wished real life could be more like this game. "Okay, Becky, just breathe . . . good . . . good . . . keep breathing—that's it! Great job! Now, just relax and feel good about yourself! Ready . . . when you get to your problems—here they come—just meet 'em head on . . . just give 'em a good whack! Good effort, Becky! Keep it up!"

When the team was being formed a few weeks ago, Becky's feminist instincts led her to favor more aggressive names than the Cosmic Comets. Her favorite names were the Queen Bees, the Amazon Warriors, and the Queen Cobras. The girls on the team, the coaching staff, and the fans did have their aggressive moments, but now she liked the way it was balanced with goodwill and unqualified support. As she was thinking this, though, Claire's friend, Melanie, took a hard grounder on the shin as she stood at first base. Amazingly, the game continued on around her, with her hopping on one foot near first base, with half of the Comets' fans yelling, "Melanie's hurt! Stop the game! Stop the game! Melanie's hurt!" They did catch on, finally, and stop the game to get Melanie out, but she could hear the Rugrats' coach arguing a technicality, that since the ball touched Melanie she was out and the inning was over. Mike was arguing vigorously with the coach, who looked like a psychotic version of the young host of "Blue's Clues." Mike was saying who cared about rules like that in a game like this, especially when a girl was hurt, and, besides, if he was really worried about it, she was touching the base when the ball hit her, so she couldn't be out. Becky could hear Hannah Robinson saying in disgust a few rows behind her about the Rugrats' coach, "What's *his* problem! A man like that shouldn't be around girls in the first place. Does he think this is the World Series? He needs to get a life!"

The ugly interlude was soon over on the field, but it soured the mood at the game considerably. Becky had completely lost track of the outcome of the argument, although Mike was clearly the champion of common sense and compassion. He seemed to fit the role well tonight, and that just completely caught Becky off guard. For some reason, this scene, and her looking at his well proportioned body, made her think of an article she had started in the latest *O* magazine about the nature of sexuality in men and women. The detail that intrigued her the most was the claim that testosterone, both in men *and* women, was the chemical trigger for *all* sexual feelings. At least that's what she thought it said. That seemed so odd, but if it were true, she figured she had a very sizable load of testosterone, too, especially lately! Before she could figure it all out and continue reading, she had to intercept Jack chasing their cat, Molly, with an oversized red plastic bat, yelling, "Sword fight! Sword fight!" As she swept him off his feet in mid-flight, he cheerfully challenged her, "Sword fight! Sword fight, Mama! Sword fight now!"

On the field, the poor sportsmanship by their coach seemed to take the spunk right out of the Rugrats' team, although they maintained a 13-11 lead as the game wound quickly down. The one-hour time limit seemed like an incredibly reasonable and humane rule for these games, Becky was thinking, as she planned her escape from the game with Ruby, Jack, and her granddad somehow herded together still intact. Also, she had to gather up Claire and get her in the van. Now the girls from each team were forming lines and high-fiving each member on the opposing team in a steady, moving procession. This seemed like another very civilized aspect of the game. Tracy was saying to Becky, "I'm completely exhausted! The girls did great. . . . Claire is so fast I can't get over it—Stacy! Over here, hon!"

When Becky looked over to where Jack and her granddad were, she was shocked to see Claire leading them by the hand over to her. It looked like some kind of New Age Norman Rockwell painting with Claire in her Comets' T-shirt, until she saw Mike walking behind them a few steps, congratulating other girls and their parents as he went.

Having Mike nearby made Becky very nervous and shy. She hugged Claire a little self-consciously in front of him and said, "Claire, we're so proud of you! How did you get so good! You played just great . . . you—"

"Mom," Claire cut in, "Dad's taking us all to TCBY . . . Dad and Mr. Johnson. Okay, Mom . . . ?"

Mike, hanging back, and acting sort of shy, regretful, and humble in a way that Becky had never seen before, said, "I can have her back soon, Becky . . ." Then he walked over to Ruby and gave her a big hug, saying, "How are you, sweetie girl!" Ruby was squirming around in his hug, but she had this huge, cockeyed smile on her face.

Becky's granddad broke up this love fest, saying, "Well, *I'm* the one whose cob-dam ice cream's in the dumper! Can't say I'm surprised, either! Why stop now!"

That got everyone moving, with Mike scooping Jack from the ground and simultaneously tossing him several feet up in the air and catching him. Jack was squealing in delight as they all walked toward the parking lot together. It seemed like a happy scene, but something about it felt completely wrong, like that shocked feeling when she thought Jack was missing.

Before the break up two years ago, Becky often thought that she did most of the hard every day work with the kids and that generally Mike could pick and choose the good times to interact with them. She knew it wasn't quite so simple as this, but it seemed like the basic truth. Oddly, she didn't feel like this now. This wasn't an easy time for Mike with the kids, yet he was handling it in a dignified and caring way. He had stirred up some admiration for himself in Becky, against all her expectations. Becoming the sole guardian of her grandfather the last two years, while simultaneously caring for Jack, Ruby, and Claire, had toughened an already tough Becky to the point that this pinprick of sympathy and tenderness for Mike shocked her. And thinking about the break up, of course, reminded her of her mother's death, as did so many things. She still couldn't get over it. The world just seemed incomplete without her mom—it just didn't seem right or possible that such a vital person could die in the prime of her life, but Becky was proud of the way she held things together, impossibly, just like her mom.

The whole deal about Mike taking Claire and the other girls to TCBY had been worked out quickly with gestures and whispers, since Becky didn't want to get Jack and her granddad riled up about ice cream right before their bedtimes. This had been Claire's night; Becky wasn't going to undercut it now. She knew she gave Claire a lot of adult responsibility, especially in helping with Jack and her granddad; she obviously needed some time to be a kid, as well.

On the ride back home in the van, Jack and Becky's granddad were in great spirits listening to Jack's tapes. The van was rocking as her granddad belted out "There Was an Old Woman Who Swallowed a Fly" along with the tape. Becky thought there ought to be more old songs like that with old *men* doing stupid, funny stuff like that, but Jack thought the tape was almost unbearably funny. She was always amazed at how much rhythm and musical sense he had. Like many other things, it just seemed to be hardwired in his body somehow.

At home, Becky put Ruby to bed first while Jack and her granddad played with the wooden train track set up on a table in the living room. One time, as she listened to them downstairs to make sure everything was okay, she overheard her granddad telling Jack, "Now don't tell your mama this, bud, but I know a lot about trains from the inside out, if you know what I mean . . ."

"Thomas!" Jack replied, "Thomas the Train! Thomas! Train!"

"Yeah, well, maybe . . . but, ya know, a fella could get hurt jumpin' trains. Cob-bam bulls! Cob-dam greenback dollar! But, ya know, a fella could take a drink now and then, if he had it! Ya know, Jack, I wish I had some whiskey right here, right now! A fella needs a break now an' then. . . ." Before long, the two were making trains sounds together, and when they heard a train off in the distance, they nearly went through the roof, like the train had heard them and was answering their call.

Becky started the nightly routine, and first changed Jack's diaper and dressed him for bed in his bedroom and then worked on her granddad. He had gotten in the routine of all this, Depends and all, and that was a lucky thing, because Becky had had a devil of a time with him when she started taking care of him after her mom got so sick a few years back.

She sat between Jack and her granddad on Claire's old bed, which had been set up in Jack's room, and read them the book *Noisy Nora*. Jack, of course, loved the fact that the baby mouse in the book was named Jack, and the book was a general favorite of both Jack and her granddad. "Jack had dinner early, Father played with Kate, Jack needed burping, so Nora had to wait . . ." Jack soon caught on to the refrain ". . . so Nora had to wait . . ." and began chiming in "Wait!" every time each refrain ended. Likewise, he caught on to the repetition of "'Nora!' said her sister, 'Why are you so dumb?'" and jumped in exactly on the beat with "Dumb!" Jack was in ecstasy when Nora slammed doors and banged windows to get attention, and especially when she purposely poured marbles all over the kitchen floor. Of course, he yelled out "Marbles!" just from seeing the picture, before Becky could read the page. Her granddad's cynicism faded completely during the reading. Among others things, Becky wondered if the old-fashioned lifestyle pictured in the book reminded him of his childhood.

Whatever the reason, *Noisy Nora* was a book he could always get completely behind. When she finished the book, and had let Jack proclaim, "The End!" her granddad gave her a sentimental little lip-trembling hug and said, "Love ya, baby!"

Since Jack was far less likely to get in big trouble now than her granddad (six or eight months ago, it had pretty much been a toss up), she put her granddad down for the night first, then Jack. Both went down as easy as pie, and that was rare, indeed. Jack, in fact, was as sensitive and sweet as he could be, hugging her and kissing her, and saying, "Ma-ma! Ma-ma! Ma-ma!" over and over again, as if he had zeroed in on the special, sweet secret of the universe. The fact was, she could admit now that things had calmed down, he was the sweetest, most sensitive boy she had ever seen, as well as the rowdiest, and the usual ratio was that fifty percent of the time he was sensitive and fifty percent of the time he was a berserk, macho monster. Now, she would see if Jack and her granddad and Ruby stayed down for the night. The hard part, at any rate, was over.

When Mike brought Claire home, it was a little awkward because Claire raced upstairs to go to bed and left them alone. They made awkward small talk for a few minutes, and then Mike said, and he seemed like a nervous high school boy on a date, sort of scuffing his tennis shoes on the floor, "Becky, I don't know how you do it with these kids! You just do a great job! Claire is just so mature . . . and granddad, I think I'm going to have to have a fistfight with him every time I see him—I just don't know how you handle them all! Becky . . . I just wanted to give you a hug before I left. . . ."

Becky liked the Mike she was seeing now, but he had never been a hugging kind of guy, so she was on the alert for any trick he might be pulling. She let him walk over and hug her. It was a gentle and tender hug, and seemed genuine, with no ulterior motives. When he just turned to walk quickly and shyly away, whispering, "Goodnight . . . ," she was caught so by surprise she grabbed for his hand.

One thing led to another, and, forty minutes later, the two were in her bed upstairs listening to Ruby bounce with glee on her bed in the bedroom next door. It seemed comfortable somehow with Mike now for Becky, and somehow very awkward, as well. For her survival and the survival of her children, she had written him out of her life, and she had never imagined any scenario like this, let alone thought it through. She was thinking it through now, though, because, once again, her life and the life of her family seemed to depend on it.

She and Mike had come to an obvious stopping point, there, naked in her bed, listening to Ruby vigorously bounce and squeal on her bed like there was no tomorrow. Becky knew she had to decide something now, one way or the other, so she started doing just that, not really knowing what she would say or how she would say it. "Mike," she said, "you know we've got to start over completely. I mean *completely*, from the beginning. Maybe we have started over . . . in a way."

"I know, Becky . . . I know . . ."

"Mike, I don't think you *do* know. I don't think you realize the serious trouble we were in before—how close our lives were to being ruined . . . completely . . . forever. . . . "You can't stay here tonight. We have to start over—from the beginning."

"Becky, I *do* know . . . it's just that your standards are so high!" he said, a little exasperated.

"I know, Mike—they've had to be high because yours were always so low!" She braced herself for what had to come next.

He seemed to fight back a shudder, leaned over and kissed her softly on the cheek, and said, "We can start over . . . I'll try. . ." He grabbed his clothes and gave her a goofy little embarrassed grin as he headed off to put on his clothes and to leave for the night.

Because of that, she wanted him to stay, but she still knew he had to leave. They had tried the unconscious approach to love before, and it seemed to ruin a great part of Becky's life. This time they had to do it with their eyes wide open to have any chance at all. Becky had always thought of Mike as one of her children, in a sense. Although she knew he had many outstanding qualities as a man, he just didn't take complete responsibility for his life, and certainly not for their life as a family. And, without any doubt, he was her hardest child to handle, and the most wayward, although Jack and her granddad might have given him a run for his money lately.

The way he had acted the last few weeks, especially today, and especially tonight, he didn't seem to Becky like her child, or anybody's child, although there was still a helpless quality about him. She thought he would explode when she asked him to leave; she just knew she was in for some awful, terrible, unbelievable scene when he brought up her high standards. But, no, the look she had seen as he left told her that he was growing up in a hurry.

Christmas Candy, Sex, Death, and Love

As she approached forty, one thing Becky Hawkins had never before associated with Christmas Eve was earth-shaking sex in the afternoon. As she walked out the door into a frigid blast and headed for the family van, she smiled, relishing the last few giddy months with her husband, Mike, careful not to fall on the icy front porch steps. In their life-and-death struggle all of her adult life, they had never really gotten it right before the last six months or so. Now, ironically, as they shared their feelings—and bodies—their feelings expanded to fill everything. This kind of love unlocked the door to both tenderness and sexual passion. Becky was just thinking how she felt like she had just gone over Niagra Falls and was now floating in calm water, when she heard the sound of her three-year-old son, Jack, high above her, "Hi, Mom! Look! I over the edge!"

The universe stood still in that instant, except for Becky's heart, which jerked sideways violently. She looked up to see her son leaning over the snow-covered balcony twenty-five feet above where she stood. The top of the short balcony wall was wide, and he leaned on and over the wall, with his feet apparently on one of the lawn chairs up there. He called out again, happily, "Hi, Mom! I need to see that tree. I need to get on the roof!"

She didn't scream. One small voice inside her urged calm and seemed to advise her, "You have only one chance to save your son's life: stay calm, get him moving backwards." "Jack," she called up hurriedly, shocked at how matter-of-fact she sounded, "go back inside, now—I've got candy for you!"

Becky was headed inside, picking up speed as she was hidden on the front porch from Jack's sight, when she heard Jack call back, "Can-dy! For *me*!"

The door was flung open in Becky's wake, and she was taking the steps to the second floor two at a time, her knee-length boots with the big heels not slowing her down one bit. She checked the door to the balcony ten times a day. No child could work that old skeleton key. It didn't make sense. If Mike had unlocked that door to string up icicle lights . . .

She tore through the hall and then through Ruby's bedroom and out to the balcony to scoop up Jack, who had only made it down from the lawn chair and was stamping down little sections of the six-inch deep snow on the wooden slats of the balcony floor. She grabbed him so fiercely that he was startled. She seemed to be hugging him desperately and shaking him angrily at the same time. The hugging soon won out, and she hugged him so hard and so long, he complained, "Mom . . . you're hurting my body!"

She eased up and held him so that she could look at him and talk to him. "Jack," she said, "I love you more than anything, but," and now the anger was taking over, "I'm so mad at you. You could have killed yourself!"

She took him back inside and closed and locked the balcony door, putting the key in her pocket (already mentally hiding it behind the spices on the top self of the kitchen cabinet above the stove). She squatted down to his eye-level as he stood by the glass-paned balcony door. She could feel the cold wetness on his sweater from the ledge of the balcony wall. She gripped his shoulders and tried to shake her message home, "Don't you ever, ever, ever go out on that balcony again! Do you hear me! Never, ever, ever! Do you promise?"

"I promise," Jack said. He always seemed sincere when he said this, but Becky knew he understood the formula. He just didn't seem to get that he had been in danger.

She said, "Show me how you got out there. Was it this handle? Was it the key?" But she didn't even want to show him the key, to give him any ideas, in case it wasn't the key. "Was the door unlocked—did you just turn the handle, or did you have to turn the key? I need to know."

Jack kind of shrugged and said, "I worked and worked, Mom. I used the handle. I used the key. I made it open."

She just couldn't get it straight in his mind how serious all this was, or in hers what exactly had happened, and she became increasingly exasperated trying to convince him he would have died, and what that meant, or that he would have been severely injured, and what that meant. Finally, she said, "Okay, think about this. You sneak out on the balcony—however you did it. You fall off. You're dead . . . lying in the snow. I'm crying. Your dad is crying. Claire is crying. Granddad is crying. You're lying in the snow, dead. Your body is cold and blue. [He perks up on the "blue" part, but Becky won't stop and let him get started on that tangent.] You'll never do one happy thing again. No candy. No *Justice League*. No SpongeBob. No Hot Wheels. You're lying there dead, in the snow . . . tonight Santa flies right over our house. No point in stopping—ever again—Jack's dead! No toys from Santa!"

A wail went up from Jack with that. Bingo! "No toys . . . from Santa!" he moaned, miserable, completely stricken. Jack's instant crying switch was turned on, too, at that instant.

"Jack . . . Jack . . . Jack . . . you didn't fall, you didn't die, you'll get your toys from Santa, but now you're starting to get the picture. You disobey your mom—I've told you, and told you, and told you: don't go out on that balcony. *Not ever!* You disobey your mom . . . you go out on the balcony when your mom says no . . . you fall, you kill yourself . . . that's absolutely right: no toys from Santa, not tomorrow, not ever."

The thoughts flickered across Jack's face as he worked through this, then a hint of relief, "Oh, man! What was I thinking!"

Becky was so happy at this, because that was their secret phrase for all the stupid, foolish, thoughtless things people do that are bound to turn out badly. "What was he *thinking?* What was she *thinking?* What was I *thinking?*"

And then it hit Becky. "Jack, weren't you supposed to be taking a nap? How long have you been up?"

"Mom . . ." Jack complained, "my candy. . . ."

Becky paid up, fishing out a worn-looking cherry Starburst, hoping the wrapper hadn't permanently embedded itself in the candy. She tried to keep these bribes handy, if her clothing would allow that inconspicuously. In principle, she was very much against both candy and bribes, but every month or two she would use a bribe as the lesser evil. "Jack," she said, "here's your candy. Candy is so bad for you. It just totally messes up your immune system."

Jack, agreed, saying, "This is way, way, way too much sugar," as he happily popped the candy in his mouth and started to chew.

Becky's life often seemed to her like that old riddle about the fox and the goose and the corn and getting them safely across the river when you could only take one at a time. Of the five people Becky took care of, three of them basically needed one adult supervising them at all times. Ruby certainly fit in that category. Her eighty-nine-year-old grandfather often fit in that category, as did Jack. As he neared the age of four, Jack was somewhat more manageable, but he had always seemed a greater challenge to Becky than other boys she observed the same age. Even a year or two ago, the same-aged boys of her friends and relatives seemed to orbit peacefully near their mothers, whereas Jack seemed to break free of her gravitational pull in an instant. She kept thinking, "This is a good sign, *if* he can survive!" Claire could be a great help, and so could Mike. Well, Mike was a terrific help now, when he wasn't at work, but, she remembered how, for a great part of their past, he seemed like the only child it aggravated her to care for. Somehow, she had to juggle the endless schedules for school, work, day care, and therapists. She could do it, but it was hard for her not to feel there was a loose thread somewhere.

She was thinking something along this line when she strode into the kitchen with Jack balanced on her hip like old times—he was really getting too big for her to carry like this. The most sacred household time of any holiday or weekend—naptime—had already been profaned, so she had decided to get on with the day. A cartoon show was on in the kitchen. Anyone who might watch cartoons, including her granddad, was supposed to be taking a nap, but having a cartoon show in the kitchen at any time of the day didn't surprise her. That was more or less expected, but what was unexpected was the odd way her granddad lay with his head on the kitchen table. Something was definitely wrong with this picture, and her heart jerked sideways in her chest again. He was too still . . . he didn't seem to be breathing. His mouth gaped open in a hideous, weird shape, pressed flat by the table. "Granddad . . . !" she called as she walked quickly up to him.

Her call produced a slight quiver in his face. That seemed to her a very hopeful sign. As she got closer, she started to notice a sharp smell, out of place in the kitchen. As she was starting to place the smell in her mind, she noticed the brown bottle on the floor by his chair. It was a bottle of brandy someone had brought to a party at their house a week or so before. She thought she had hidden it in a granddad-proof way behind boxes of cereal and plastic forks in a lower cabinet, but apparently she hadn't succeeded.

As she stooped and picked up the bottle, which was quite a struggle still holding Jack, and put it on the kitchen table, Jack exclaimed, "That's alcohol!" He was quite a Puritan when it came to drinking and smoking, and Becky was glad. When Becky read him *101 Dalmatians*, he was a little concerned about Cruella de Vil's plan to use the puppies to make fur coats, but he was absolutely outraged and mortified that she smoked cigarettes!

Jack's exclamation woke up his great-granddad, who looked bleary and completely lost at first. He couldn't quite seem to place Jack or Becky or the bottle of brandy sitting next to him, but something on the TV caught his attention, and he grinned up at Jack and said, in that funny, gruff doggy voice used on the cartoon, "Scooby-Dooby-Doo!" and gave Jack a high five.

"Granddad," Becky said, picking up the bottle of brandy for emphasis, "did you open that balcony door! Jack was just out on that balcony, and he could have killed himself!"

Something in her tone obviously hit a nerve. "'Becca," he said angrily, and slurring a little, "you've been a good girl, but *don't* you go shitting on my roof! I won't have it!" he said, and slammed his fist down on the formica of the kitchen table. "I'm too old for that game!"

Jack was delighted, saying, "Granddad said 'poo-poo'! He said 'poop'! He said, 'Poop on the roof'! Why did he say 'poop on the roof'? Granddad said 'shi—'"

"Jack . . . !" Becky said, holding her hand up like a cop signaling a stop to all potty-mouth behavior, not that she'd had much luck in that department lately. "Jack, you don't have to imitate *only* bad behavior. You're alive, but you're headed for a spanking!" Becky knew she was in the proverbial no-win situation. She scooted a chair up beside her granddad for Jack and angled him into it. Holding the bottle of brandy up for emphasis, like she was the Statue of Liberty, she said, "Fine! Why don't you boys have a big bucket of sugar and a big bucket of brandy and watch cartoons all afternoon. Just sit there and don't move, either one of you!" Jack and her granddad seemed to want to respond and defend themselves, but the sight and sound of Shaggy and Scooby being chased by some moaning green ghost down a long hall had stolen their attention, although, once she headed out of the kitchen, she could hear her granddad confide in Jack, "You know, a bucket 'o brandy don't sound half bad, bud!"

Becky quickly went upstairs to check on Ruby, who was supposed to be taking a nap, too, but, at the rate things were going, Ruby would be out on the roof by now, although with Ruby a simple tumble down the stairs was the ultimate nightmare. Becky could hear Ruby's bedsprings going, so she knew Ruby was bouncing up and down. Ruby was deliriously happy and bouncing in a wild and vigorous way. She bounced from her knees, so it wasn't terribly dangerous, but even a fall from her bed, and these happened with a dreadful regularity, every couple of weeks, could be devastating for Ruby. Over the years, many of Becky's most profound fears concerning Ruby were simply put on "hold." Would she ever talk? Would she ever be potty trained? Who knew? Maybe not. Probably not. If she were like this at age nine, after all that effort and expense, all that therapy and education, what would she be like at age thirteen or seventeen or twenty-one? Who knew? More and more Becky was just glad to see her happy. Ruby clearly understood a great deal. She took a lot in, so what if not much could come out? More and more, even in public, Becky was just happy (well, mostly) if Ruby were happy. And at this moment, Ruby seemed about as happy as any human being could get. She was happy before Becky came in and even happier now that Becky had. There was an old clapping rhythm that Becky had always used with Ruby over the years to get her excited and creeping (as the medical experts they followed described it) fast on her hands and knees when she was two years old or later walking fast in the park. Becky found herself doing that now, even throwing in the old "Go, Ruby, go!" in rhythm to Ruby's repetitive gymnastics on her bed. Ruby was shrieking and squealing so loudly Becky was afraid it would wake up Mike, but the household was used to hearing things like this from Ruby at any time of day or night, and there was no point in trying to shush Ruby, anyway, so Becky just fanned the flames awhile. Finally, Ruby flopped down on the bed so happy she could hardly contain herself. Becky hugged her cheek against Ruby's cheek for a second, although Ruby never really stopped moving for this, and said, "Ruby, you're a special, beautiful girl, and you know it, don't you! We're so lucky to have you! I think this is going to be your best Christmas ever, so you better rest up a little more this afternoon." This pep talk seemed to inspire Ruby to give bouncing on her bed one more try; Becky could hear the bed springs as she hurried back down the stairs to get Jack and her granddad for a last quick trip to the mall. She knew this was a suicidal venture in the middle of the afternoon on Christmas Eve, but the last piece of the Christmas shopping puzzle was a top that Claire wanted from Abercrombie, and Becky was determined to complete her mission (of course, there would be present wrapping and toy assembling tonight after the kids were in bed).

Becky had swooped down on Jack and her granddad so quickly and gotten them in the van so quickly they never knew what hit them. They zoomed past the nativity scene in front of the McDonald's on the way to the mall. Jack had asked her about this when it was put up after Thanksgiving. Becky had said, "That's Jesus," to which Jack had responded, "Chuckie Cheese's?!" Explaining the baby, the parents, the cows and sheep, and the shepherds took quite a bit of doing! Now, stuck in traffic on the way to the mall, Jack said a line he'd heard recently from *Stuart Little II*, "George doesn't know poop from applesauce!" This allusion to the movie they'd watched together had both Jack and her granddad in hysterics. Becky never knew which way her granddad would go on any issue. Whatever syndrome was monkeying with his brain was doing so in a seemingly random pattern. One minute he was the Marquis De Sade, the next Cotton Mather, and the next Jimmy

Stewart. Sometimes he egged on Jack's poo-poo talk, sometimes he was outraged and self-righteous, and sometimes he topped such talk with bizarre and colorful language of his own. Now the two were trading poo-poo witticisms. Granddad: "George doesn't know poop from artichokes. George doesn't know poop from rutabagas. George doesn't know poop from Minneapolis. . . ." Jack: "George doesn't know poop from peanut butter. George doesn't know poop from pancakes. George doesn't know poop from tricycles." Becky knew she fluctuated as much as her granddad did on this subject. She went from fury, to moral outrage, to apathy, to practical advice: "Jack, if you talk like this at school, you're going to get in so much trouble. People don't want to hear a three-year-old talk like that. Some parents would spank you and spank you and spank you until you stopped. Jack, I never want to hit you again. I never spanked Claire, not once. Why can't you just help your mother?"

At this moment, Becky was in an apathetic mood concerning the poo-poo talk, bracing herself for the pre-mall traffic, the mall parking lot, and the mall itself, and getting Jack and her granddad into Abercrombie and back out again. Claire had skipped this poo-poo talking phase entirely, but she had also skipped all the other swaggering, slamming the wall, acting defiant, jumping off the roof, sword fighting, shooting, screaming bloody murder, car-crash-loving phases, as well.

Last night, Becky, among other books, had read Jack a beautifully illustrated version of *The Night Before Christmas*. Becky absolutely loved the artwork. One frame shows the narrator in his night cap looking up out the window of a very realistic huge old New England house. The next frame shows Santa and his sleigh making that arcing turn way up in the night sky above the houses and the snowy countryside, as they begin the descent for a landing. Of course, Jack was all over this one, doing one of his poo-poo rants. Did Santa go poop? Did the reindeer go poop? Santa's going poo-poo down the chimney. Poo-poo in your eyes, poo-poo in your hair, poo-poo in your ears, poo-poo in your mouth, poo-poo in your sleigh, poo-poo in the bag slung over your shoulder. At least Dr. Seuss never got ahold of this idea, although Jack recently twisted one of his books into *Green Eggs and Poo-Poo*.

Becky had fought this poo-poo battle for about six weeks. She was sure it would end, and it couldn't end soon enough to suit her. She had used spanking (although she didn't "believe in" spanking). She had tried threats and loss of rewards. She had tried early bedtimes. She had tried tons of straightforward discussion and practical advice. Of course, threatening "talking to your father about this" was the perfect and frequent last resort, but even that threat, even that actuality, didn't work perfectly or for very long. Mainly, she had resigned herself to fighting this talk in public, and mostly letting it go otherwise. She always jumped in, every single time, with advice, threats, corrections, and punishments, but she just couldn't keep it up. He was winning this one. Still, she knew his superego was fairly well developed. He would charm the Parents as Teachers supervisor who would come to test him at their house, and then say to Claire's teacher upon first meeting her at Parent-Teacher night, "You're poop!" Of course, he picked his spots for those guerrilla hit-and-run raids, because retaliation was always sure, softened only by the number of witnesses and the lack of sound proofing in the nearest restroom.

Two days ago, Jack had acquired a remarkable artifact that seemed to jibe with all his poo-poo talk. Becky still couldn't quite believe it, even when she was looking right at it. It was a little Hot Wheels hotrod car in the shape of a gold-and-silver-plated toilet. It had the toilet bowl, the toilet seat, and a public-building-style flushing handle. About the only non-toilet thing on it were the wheels. The steering wheel was a plunger turned upside down. Apparently, the driver would sit in the toilet and drive this little hotrod toilet around. Even Jack couldn't seem to believe this toilet car, "Who could have a toi-let tar!?" Jack was doing some riff about a "super-duper poo-poo powered haircut shooter" when her granddad took one of his moralistic turns. "Jack," he said dramatically and forcefully, "you need to keep that poo-poo talk under your cap, now and forever! That poo-poo-bottom-boobie talk is a pretty straight drop to a burning hell—"

Of course, even in his quick and fiery descent, Jack said, gleefully, "Granddad said 'bottom.' Granddad said 'boobie'!"

Her granddad was a remarkably strong man who seemed as if he could turn flamboyantly violent at any second, but he was always gentle with her children, whatever his words and gestures might convey, although she always worried he would turn violent to people outside her family. He reached over and grabbed Jack's hand, saying, "You better button it up, bub, and throw away the zipper, or *your* bottom is going to get a red-hot tattoo! And I mean it!"

Jack, never one to be easily intimidated, yelled back, "No, *I* mean it!" But, before this situation could escalate any further, Becky found a lucky parking spot fairly near the mall, but had to blare the horn to keep someone from cutting in front of her.

Outside the van, she ordered, "Hold hands the whole way! No one lets go!" She put herself in the middle and one of them on each side and dodged the traffic as she plunged them into the rivers of people flooding the mall. She was thinking through the culture shock that awaited Jack and her granddad in Abercrombie's. All of those monumental-sized bare torsos were a shock even to Becky. Although Mike had, thankfully, backed off some on his exercises, he could still give those boys a run for their money. Jack had that same weird combination of swagger and innocence as those models, and Becky was shocked to realize now that she cultivated that same look for him—except with his shirt *on*—with his clothes and haircut. Claire and her friends all cultivated that look, in a diminutive way . . . well, some of her fifth-grade friends were already larger than their moms. Abercrombie seemed to be backing off, switching from those glaring color photos to nostalgic black and white ones, but what got to Becky was the commodification of all that flesh. There was an open niche in the macho naked boy market, and Abercrombie filled it. Why would boys *or* girls go for that advertising? She guess it flaunted convention . . . while selling clothes that could have come from the GAP. A funny image occurred to Becky as she pictured her granddad and Jack bare-chested and posing for Abercrombie. You couldn't get any more macho, and there was nothing phony about them; you could practically hear the testosterone sloshing around in them as they walked. But they were caricatures of masculinity; Mike was the real thing.

Becky towed her two macho salmon swimming desperately upstream through the crowd. She had parked as near Abercrombie as she could and knew exactly where the burnt-orange top Claire wanted was and where it was in the store. She had already filled everything in on the check except the amount of money. Inside, she wasn't quite prepared for the walls of bare teen-aged flesh that were the store's trademark. She was even less prepared for Jack's and her granddad's reactions. They were absolutely stunned at first, and she took full advantage of that and had the top in Claire's size and was heading for the cashier. Jack spotted enough monumental-sized photos of bottoms and boobies to get him going on that topic, but her granddad was doing a slow burn. He was staring at the twelve-foot tall bare washboard-bellied teenager on the wall next to him with a very personal malice. As they approached the clerk to pay, he said disgustedly, "Them boys need to learn to keep it in their Cob Damn pants! What church do *they* go to!" Of course, her reaction was the one she'd learned over the years with Ruby, her granddad, and Jack out in public, a bemused "What'll they think of next!" shrug, like they were such good ordinary people who always acted so normal that she couldn't imagine where this off-the-wall behavior came from. But then she saw her granddad focusing with an odd menace on the salesgirl's nose ring, eyebrow ring, and lip ring. Becky was bracing to head off the second she got the receipt. "Holy shit on the patio!" her granddad said indignantly. "What happened to your face, gal!"

Becky pulled the receipt from the stunned girl's hand, mouthing, "I'm sorry. . . ." Pulling her granddad and Jack and saying, "Granddad, I believe your holiday brandy days are over!" The bright spot in all this, and it shone like the blazing Christmas star to her, was that Jack was pulling his granddad away from the scene with great determination, sensing trouble, and trying to help out. As they gained momentum and she was pulling them and leading them away, she said to Jack, "You're a good boy, Jack (*some*times!). You're a genius! I love you!" To her granddad she said, "I love you, too, granddad, but you have to be careful with people's feelings. . . . We better get the hel—heck . . . outta Dodge!"

Zooming back home, it struck Becky she had made it through the trip with no serious bathroom complications. Neither Jack nor her granddad was someone she wanted to take into the women's restroom at the mall on Christmas Eve. Taking both of them together defied her comprehension. Still, dozens of times a week, often many times in a single day, she was faced with incredible bathroom trauma, often public, involving Ruby, her granddad, or Jack. Ruby was easily the most challenging of this group, but her granddad was gaining ground rapidly. Ruby could have intergalactic explosions at any time—out in public, in the middle of the night—and although these oceanic poo-poo storms swept all before them, Becky had to jump in, beyond all human reason and power, and deal with the situation and keep dealing with it until it was cleaned up, with minimum harm to both Ruby (both physically and mentally) and whatever environment she happened to be in. Jack actually was easy, in many ways now, but it took more time helping him go than simply changing diapers, but that was a very worthwhile trade-off in Becky's mind. Jack could talk about poo-poo all day, but Becky was the one who actually had to deal with it! Well, Mike was getting his share lately, too.

Safely back home, Becky saw an extremely unusual configuration in the kitchen: Mike, Claire, and Ruby watching TV. It turned out to be that weird 1960s cutout animation version of "Rudolph the Red-Nosed Reindeer," narrated by Burl Ives. Of course, anytime Ruby was focused on watching TV, it felt like a tremendous victory. Ruby loved the old bang-em-on- the-head cartoons. It was usually hard to tell what Ruby thought or felt, but, time after time, Becky witnessed clear examples that Ruby loved to see other people (even fictional ones) getting hurt and getting in trouble. This seemed fairly natural to Becky, given all the suffering Ruby had gone through (why not give someone else a turn!). This is the only time Becky ever tolerated cruelty in her children (and she was the only one to realize this about Ruby, in any case). Becky always made the obvious connection of Rudolph the Red-Nosed Reindeer and handicapped children, who were shunned because they were different. Becky didn't know what was getting to Ruby in this particular show, or if she just happened to be chemically tuned-in at the moment. Maybe she liked the subtle symbolism, but there seemed to be plenty of the bang-em-on-the-head type stuff, as well. Becky noticed Claire eyeing the Abercrombie bag knowingly, so she shifted it out of Claire's sight. Mike was joking with Claire, "This Rudolph needs to get a life. He needs to focus on self-actualizing activity and not worry so much what other people—other reindeer—think!"

Of course, Claire wanted to know what "self-actualizing" was, and Jack, seeing what was on, jumped ahead to talking about his favorite part, since he'd seen it a couple of nights before. He loved the part where Charlie, the lookout for the Island of Unwanted Toys, says, "No child wants to play with a Charlie-in-a-Box!" (as opposed to a Jack-in-a-Box). Of course, Jack had had a field day with that one ever since, "No one wants to play with poop in a box! No one wants to play with a bottom in a box! No one wants to play with a weenie in a box!" Before Jack had even gotten warmed up, Mike had jerked him around by the arm and was giving him a warning stare, saying, "No one wants to play with a boy who's going to bed right now if he can't stop saying 'poop'. . . ." Becky grabbed this little bit of time to hurry up to the attic to wrap a few presents before the traditional Christmas Eve activities got underway.

By the time Becky and Mike had made it to dinner time, gotten through dinner, and prepared and transported the kids to Becky's brother Joe's house, the Hawkins family had survived enough everyday traumas to fuel a dozen sitcoms, and there was even one moment of high drama. Becky led Mike into the living room to discuss the Jack-on-the-balcony incident. Becky had thought she had been careful and sensitive in the way she brought this up, but something in her tone hit Mike as accusatory, and he was outraged. The rest of the household got to hear him loud and clear as they listened in the kitchen. Of course, he didn't unlock the door to the balcony and leave it open! Of course, he wasn't careless enough to try to kill his only son!

The Christmas Eve ritual for Becky's family was an unusual one. Her mother had started with Becky and her other brothers and sisters more than thirty years ago, and Becky, as the oldest, was the ringleader in carrying on this tradition after her mother's death to honor her. What her mother had always done is sit all the kids down and read them Hans Christian Andersen's *The Little Match Girl*. Of course, when her mother read the story all those years ago, the kids rolled their eyes and thought it was the funniest, weirdest thing ever. They lit a lot of candles and drank egg nog, and certain children either got to strike a match at the appropriate time in the story or say "Scriiitch!" like it did in the book. Her mother always used a brittle, old, hard-to-read edition of the story. She had trouble simply getting through the words, but, as regular as clockwork, as the story neared the end and the poor little girl began to freeze to death in the streets of Copenhagen on New Year's Eve, her mother broke down crying, and had to struggle through her crying all the way to the end, where the girl lights her last match, sees her last vision, and dies, joining her grandmother in heaven.

The reason Becky wanted to carry on this tradition, and the reason the tradition stuck in the minds of all her brothers and sisters, is that it was the clearest and easiest symbol of the overwhelming depth of her mother's love for them all. Becky had bought a new, easy-to-read, beautifully illustrated version to read for this occasion every Christmas Eve after her mother's death. She hid it so that neither Ruby nor Jack could tear it up. To Becky, it was a crazy idea to read such a morbid story to children. In the new illustrated version, you could see the poor girl's bare feet in the freezing snow, and see her turn blue as she froze to death. The text actually described her body as frozen hard when she was found the next morning. Still, Becky thought this was a good history lesson about life in mid-1800s Denmark, and it *was* an extremely powerful, an unbearably powerful, story. Of course, the kids still didn't listen, and all the kids Jack's age and younger hadn't even been alive when her mom was. The story always really got to a number of those listening, especially among her brothers and sisters, and especially with the detail at the end that a shooting star always signals someone's death. Tonight, at the very start of the story, when the boy who is a bully steals the Little Match Girl's shoe (well, it was her dead mother's shoe), and insults her to boot, yelling back as he ran that he'd keep the shoe to use as a cradle for one of his children, it was so big, she could hear Jack saying, hilariously, he thought, "Poop, poop, Christmas-tree poop!" Someone got to him quickly and shushed him, but it sure wasn't Mike, who was with a couple of the men a few rooms away drinking spiked egg nog. Her granddad slept on a couch with his head thrown back and his mouth open hugely. Ruby was curled up miserably near the Christmas tree, completely annoyed and restless, despite the care and tenderness lavished on her by Becky's sisters and others. Becky knew these party scenes were hard on Ruby, and Becky had turned sour on the whole Christmas ordeal and was ready for the torture to stop and the regular new year to begin!

Back home, Becky was relieved that Mike was getting Ruby ready for bed. Jack was easier, but she was thinking that, for the next thirty or forty minutes, she couldn't think one thought of her own, and *then* she had to wrap all the presents and get the stockings hung up, and they had to put together that gigantic new castle for Jack. As usual, she let him pick the two books. He picked *Hansel and Gretel*, and then he completely shocked her by picking a book he'd found in the bookshelves in Ruby's room, the book on Leonardo da Vinci from the *Getting to Know the World's Great Artists* series. That choice perked her up a bit. That was something different! She had created a sanitized version of *Hansel and Gretel* for Jack. She absolutely could not face even the Little Golden Books version. The cruel stepmother, to save a little food for herself because of hard times, sends the two children out in the woods to face certain death. There they meet an old woman who wants to fatten them up and eat them! She knew quite a number of mothers, even stepmothers, very well, and she had paid close attention in her psychology classes. This seemed like a story written (or told, she guessed, originally) by a man! And *Snow White*. And *Cinderella*. The most horrible part to Becky was the part, pictured very evocatively in the book, when the wicked witch, who is keeping Hansel in a cage to fatten him up to eat, is feeling his finger (really a chicken bone Hansel is using to trick her) to see if he's plump enough to eat yet. Becky noted the subtle way the artwork in the book shifted. The kindly old woman, plump and inviting before, has sprouted terrible long, sharp fingernails and a long, sharp nose and chin as she stands, in satanic anticipation, before the raging oven fire. Becky had always talked to Jack about all the kindly older women they both knew and speculated that maybe this old woman was lonely in the woods and wildly misunderstood, but not long ago, Claire or Mike or somebody had read Jack the unexpurgated version. Even though he now knew all about pushing the wicked witch into the oven, Becky still liked to speculate with him about how a good woman might go bad all alone out there in the German woods.

The book on Leonardo da Vinci took another turn with Jack than Becky expected. She thought he'd gravitate toward the ancient helicopter and submarine and machine gun drawings. No, it was the paintings of the naked baby Jesus that caught his eye. What she read was, "Leonardo was one of the first artists to paint the mother of Jesus smiling and playing with her baby. Before this, artists showed Jesus and his mother looking very serious."

Becky thought this was one of the most beautiful and insightful historical passages she'd ever read, but what Jack said was, "Is he naked?" . . . "Yes." "Does he have a bottom?" . . . "Yes, you can see it there." "Does he go pee-pee?" . . . "Yes, all people go pee-pee, Jack. Maybe he needs a diaper." "Does he fly?" . . . "No, Jack, that's a halo. Halos back then showed someone who was divine [she knew he didn't know what "divine" was], or someone blessed by the divine [she knew *she* didn't know what that meant], maybe someone who is very good." She knew she had gotten in way over her head theologically and historically. "Well, actually, I think he *can* fly, in a sense, but it's not because of the halo, and don't you ever, ever, *ever* think *you* can fly, and get on the roof. . . ."

They started going through the book casually. She would read some, then they would talk and look at pictures. This leisurely approach *did* actually give her a little time to think her own thoughts. One painting, especially, got her thinking. It showed two mothers and two babies. At first, her perception was totally jarred. She couldn't tell Jesus and Mary from the other mother and baby. She looked for the mother wearing blue, she looked for the halo, but something just seemed out of kilter. Finally, it started coming together for her, the baby Jesus was positioned higher, of course, and then she noticed the less elevated baby bowing his head and clasping his hands, praying to the other, basically identical-looking, baby. She just couldn't wrap her mind around it. What about the mothers! How did they fit in? Then she thought about the gospel singer on one of her favorite Christmas CDs singing the lyrics, "Let's Make a Baby King!" These lyrics always made her laugh. The symbolism was beautiful: the arrogance and power of Rome vs. the humility and love represented by the baby. And the baby won! The baby conquered the entire empire in a few hundred years' time, and it wasn't even a close fight! That *was* a miracle, a revolution beyond imagination. But "Let's make a baby king!" What a nutty idea. Jack would be the world's worst king, yet an incomparably better king than he would have been a year ago. Now Claire, as a young child, had the kind of perfect compassion for all living things that would make her a great queen. But, of course, she had to learn to talk and walk and read and do math before she had much of a shot at being an effective queen. Let's make a baby king?! While we're at it, let's make a dog Collector of Revenue! Let's make Herod the Great the Director of Head Start! Whoever thought of making a baby king was definitely not the mother of a little boy! She said, "Jack, do you think a baby would make a good king?"

And he responded, "Poo-poo king. Poo-poo, loo-poo. Baby poo-poo." Jack was delighted at his royally clever pronouncements.

After Becky had put Jack to bed, with visions of whirling, flashing Space Goblins emitting authentic shooting sounds as they surfed on top of their InterStellar Death Craft dancing in his head, she peeked in on him in the dark after she'd been wrapping presents and building his castle for an hour or so. Asleep, lying on his back with his head toward the foot of the bed, he was the perfect vision of childhood sweetness and innocence. Becky knew this was no illusion. During his lifetime, he had said, "I love you, Mom," fifty times as often as he had said "poo-poo." He was a wildly loving, gentle, intelligent boy—sometimes . . . a solid majority of the time, in fact, but a significant part of the time he was raw testosterone power demanding, "Me, Me, Me!" Either way, she knew, he was a wonderful gift, and the love of her life . . . along with Ruby, Claire, Mike, her granddad, and her mother.

In the old Coca-Cola ads, after the parents have tackled and tamed the impossible chore of Christmas Eve gift wrapping, they relax and bask in the glow of a job well done and the anticipation of the coming fulfillment of Christmas day. By 11:00 p.m. this night, however, Becky and Mike looked like they had barely survived a horrendous war-time ambush. And, of course, trouble had been brewing between them since Becky began lashing out about Jack's being on the balcony and nearly killing himself, with Mike lashing back. The Christmas Eve party at Joe's further fueled this fire, and all the present wrapping fanned the flames, as well. Becky offered a subtle make-up hug after she'd looked out at the treacherous balcony one more time, all lit up with strings of white Christmas lights (all those plug-ins buried in the snow adding a new, incalculable risk Becky hadn't even considered before).

Mike, of course, didn't feel he'd done anything to need to "make up" for, and only participated in the hug with a slight resistance. Becky said to him, pulling away, "I'd appreciate it if you'd watch Jack when I'm not able to. I was trying to read at the party tonight—while you were drinking with your buddies—and Jack was running wild, driving everyone crazy."

Becky didn't anticipate Mike's slamming his fist against the bedroom door and saying very dramatically, but in a genuine rage, "Becky, I work for you and our kids all day . . . every day."

Becky couldn't believe it. After these last few months, here they went again! She had started to sob already as Mike continued, "I'll be damned if I won't take a drink with my 'buddies'—your family!—on Christmas Eve! You don't get it! No one *ever* paid attention to your mother when she read that book! That was the fun of it! Kids took this solemn occasion and didn't pay attention, and rolled their eyes and made fun of her, and ran around and raised hell, while your father drank spiked egg nog! They loved her for that! She didn't expect any different—well, she did, but that was the fun of it! You've got to stop taking yourself so damn serious!"

"Mike," she said, pulling out the argument she didn't know she'd had ready for weeks, "you do work hard all day, every day, for us, but you don't take any responsibility for our family. You're a grown man! You have to take responsibility for this family, too!" Becky was crying now, hard. Something about her crying felt so right and so calming.

That is, until she spotted that old rage in Mike. She didn't realize it could still be there. She could see that, at this moment, he seemed capable of anything, any extreme violence. He seemed ready to rip that old mirror off their dresser and hurl it out the window. He was just shaking with rage, with the veins bulging at his neck and his fists clenched. He seemed capable of any atrocity. He was coming toward her. He was ready to grab her and started to, but right on the brink of the most awful and hurtful thing he could do, he seemed, visibly, to restrain himself, and, finally, to take a step back, and pull himself back together.

"Becky . . ." Mike said, "you've never understood." A sad, gentle, regretful expression, like he was giving up something important forever, took over his face. "I guess I never understood it, either. Becky, I'm *not* responsible—like you say. . . . I can't be. . . ." He paused so long, she thought he was through speaking for the night, but, finally, he continued, "At work—when they give us a chance, anyway—we try to pick the people who know what they're doing to be the responsible ones. Becky, you picked this life, every detail of it. I can't be responsible for the life you picked."

Becky answered back hatefully, amazed, "They're your kids, too, Mike. That is so sick, so selfish, what you're saying—"

"No, no . . . Becky, I mean—"

"Just leave, then! Go away . . . abandon us . . . again!"

"Becky, I've never abandoned you—" Saying this, he gripped her upper arm, trying to turn her to face him and to get her to let him finish his thought, but she angrily slapped his hand away.

"Becky . . ." he said in a sad, quiet, reluctant way that caught her attention. "Becky, if *I* had been responsible for getting Ruby to walk, she probably wouldn't be walking now—let alone for the past seven years . . . if Janice had been responsible for your granddad, he would have been dead five years ago . . . if I had been responsible for potty training Jack, he might be potty trained now, and he might not. . . . Becky, I know what I'm doing at work—I have responsibilities there. I don't know what I'm doing here. . . . The best I *can* do, Becky, is help *you*. . . . You've pretended to let me decide important things a couple of times—I appreciated that. . . . Becky, if I were responsible for things, you and I and Claire would be in the Bahamas right now. No—no, I'm not fighting now. You made the wise choices . . . even with Ruby . . . even with your granddad . . . with Jack—Becky, that's all I *can* do. It doesn't matter what I *think* about it."

It was easy to see the thoughts Becky was wrestling with in her mind reflected on her face. It was a few, long, tension-filled moments until she'd wrestled with them sufficiently to speak. "Mike . . . you're right. . . . For once."

With that last phrase, his face jerked so violently back into fury that she overlaid those dangerous words with these lifesaving ones, "No, no, I mean, that makes sense—what you've said— that makes perfect sense. Thanks, Mike, for telling me." With that, she folded her arms together on his chest like she'd done a hundred times before, and hugged him tenderly, folding herself, somehow, into his chest. In the past she could sense he'd always resisted this in some mysterious way, as if this were the ultimate trap laid by feminine wiles. Of course, it was never that—it was an unconditional offer, and this time he accepted without any reservation.

Secure in his arms, Becky thought about how the power between them had shifted over the last months, since he'd come back. She thought about how the power between them was at least equal now, or, the more she thought about it, she actually held the stronger position. She thought, calm now and content, that in many ways they were equal and yet in many ways she clearly held the strength. She knew, for once, this was profoundly good cosmic management, and it comforted her to know, now, that the two of them, even her whole family, could be pulled back from the brink of disaster and death by the power of love.

Juggling Knives and Chocolate Bars

Becky Hawkins had always dreaded the day when she would have to begin dealing with her grandfather when he was naked, that is, giving him a shower and helping him go to the bathroom. At least in terms of giving him a shower, that day had finally arrived. Due to his recent fall in the shower, there could be no further delay. It was nine o'clock on Thanksgiving morning, and Becky had navigated him through getting his sweatshirt, T-shirt, pajama pants, and socks off. Once his sporty Abercrombie boxer shorts were off, she was greeted with far more information than she wanted to know about her grandfather. He had wobbled precariously getting his last foot through the leg of his red plaid boxers as Becky braced his arm with all her weight. Becky had seen a number of naked men in the course of her life. She would have given a great deal not to have her grandfather included in this select group. She couldn't entirely divert her nervous glances away from her grandfather's nakedness. She was shocked that her granddad, past ninety now, still seemed to rank fairly high on the evolutionary scale in that vulnerable area.

At that moment, from downstairs, someone, probably her son, Jack, had kicked up the volume on *The King and I*, which she had rented for Jack and her daughter Claire to watch. It was at that part of the movie when the entire chorus of the children of the Siamese king, with their teacher, Anna, burst into the song "Getting to know you . . . getting to know all about you . . ." Becky's grandfather, not yet turned and headed for the shower, began gyrating his hips and happily swaying to the music. This struck one small corner of Becky's mind as weirdly funny. The rest of Becky's mind felt out of kilter and off balance, although it seemed to her that her granddad was simply moved by a childish innocence and joy—well, maybe . . .

"Okay, Granddad," Becky said, "We need to get you in that shower before the water starts getting cold." She was steering him around toward the shower, firmly gripping his elbow, and he was still singing and humming along with the song blasting downstairs ("getting to know you, getting to know all about you . . . getting to . . . hmmm . . . hmmm . . . hmmm . . . just like you like me . . ."). Then his happy mood turned, and he shot back in frustration at being maneuvered into the shower, "Easy, Deb . . . ! It's your party. All I do is the blame-dang dirty work—but you mean well, I guess." Just like Becky and her children, her granddad was still tall, lean, and powerful, miraculously so for a man his age, and Becky knew she faced new challenges with him, mentally and physically, getting him through taking a shower under her guidance.

The shower curtain was open, and she eased him up to and over the six-inch curb that kept the water in. Like Mission Control talking an astronaut through a delicate and dangerous space walk to repair the space craft, Becky talked her grandfather through the quick shower. "Granddad, I'm going to hand you the soap. . . . Here it is. Soap good all over . . . front and back . . . then rinse all the soap off. . . ."

Other than her granddad's getting a little carried away with his soaping and scrubbing of the genital area, the shower went fairly well, and so did her getting him shaved and dressed. She had trouble getting the hang of the sideburn clipper on the electric shaver and trouble with the folds of skin on his neck and the area right under his nostrils and the crease in his chin, but the shave he was getting was incomparably better, and did less damage to his skin, than he'd been able to do for himself recently. The hardest part, as Becky had expected, was the dangerous balancing act required to get his underwear on. When his big toe got stuck in the crotch, he exclaimed, "Good night, Louise!" When he finally got his foot through, he added venomously, "Flaming shit on the damn-ball patio!" And then, regaining his humor, "Goodnight, Mrs. Calabash . . . wherever you are!"

While Becky navigated the treacherous waters of giving her grandfather his first supervised shower successfully, Mike worked through getting Ruby ready for the day. To put this challenge in everyday terms, Becky felt that the catastrophe Ruby suffered mysteriously before she was born was the equivalent to her being nearly fatally injured in a gruesome car wreck and suffering profoundly from the wreck every day of her life. As hard as this might be for Becky and her family, Becky knew it was unimaginably worse for Ruby. Becky realized many families in her family's situation would simplify their morning routine and take advantage of nursing homes and institutions or group homes for the severely disabled. Becky had studied the horrific possibilities closely, and visited the actual homes and institutions waiting for her grandfather and daughter. She decided it was easier to make such decisions if you didn't have a vivid picture of the new life waiting for your daughter and grandfather. It's true she had other sisters equally responsible for her grandfather, but her mother would have chosen her for the task—anybody, including her sisters and Becky herself and her grandfather, would choose Becky for the job. Were these two care-giving jobs easy? No, they seemed, with the rest of her responsibilities, to border on the impossible—but not so much if she just did it and didn't worry or think about it. Did it divert Becky's attention from her other two children? Absolutely! But they seemed to gain something important from their granddad and Ruby and their family's effort in their behalf. Her granddad was an incredibly self-actualized old man, she thought, and Ruby was ecstatic many, many times a day (it's true she was miserable even more). The short answer is that she loved them both, loved them completely beyond reason and qualification, just like she loved Claire, Jack, and Mike. Mike had been a lifesaver for the past few years. Unfortunately, he had developed his own heartbreaking trouble recently. Of all things, the ultimate lady-killer was having trouble with jealousy and having trouble with the basic sex act itself. He was so far gone lately that Becky decided to keep her aquatic adventures with her granddad this morning to herself.

As Becky headed downstairs with her squeaky-clean grandfather, she passed Ruby's open door. Ruby was squealing in delight, bouncing happily on her knees on her bed like it was a trampoline; she was all dressed for the day, beaming at Mike. Mike had a quirky smile and was teasing her in a singsong voice, "Ruby, you're my little snickerdoodle. . . . Work all day, work all night, and what do you get? . . . That's right . . . snickerdoodle!" Ruby had always loved Mike's voice. He had always been such a handsome, strong, sexy man, with his blondish-brown hair and unshakable confidence, but this sensitive, sustained tenderness toward their children was new, at least to Becky, in the last few years, although he'd always showed these feelings in bursts.

The most challenging chore of the day, in Becky's mind, was hosting the big noontime Thanksgiving dinner for her family. Although, since almost all the food was being brought by other family members, and Claire was preparing pan after pan of homemade dinner rolls, it was pretty smooth sailing so far. With the mammoth turkey safely roasting away in the oven, Becky thought she could work in a quick Spiderman bubble bath for Jack. He was the most macho boy she had ever seen, but he was wild about anything merchandised as "Spiderman." Spiderman bubble bath seemed like an oxymoron to Becky, like Superman cucumber sandwiches.

The Spiderman bubble bath made it easy to get Jack upstairs and undressed. Becky was always amazed at Jack's behavior once his underwear came off. He started sexual thrusting movements immediately. Somehow, his underwear (and, a few years ago, his diapers) seemed to keep this behavior contained. This morning was no exception, as he hunched his bed and waggled his bottom provocatively at Becky. This behavior seemed hard-wired into Jack, and what bothered Becky was that is seemed so adult.

As always, in almost any situation with Jack, Becky moved in with words and hands to modify his behavior. "Jack," she said as she grabbed his shoulders to maneuver him off his bed and toward the bathroom, "stop it! You better get your bath toys and get moving, or you're going to lose—"

Wrestling free of his mother, Jack stood naked on his bed, chest thrust out, and proclaimed, "It's suuu-per peee-nis . . . to the resss-cue!"

"Jack, calm down, or no Spiderman bubble bath! You need to get your toys and get in the tub right now!"

"Mom, I *am*, okay?"

"Jack, do you think Spiderman would act like that?"

This seemed to make him think a little bit. "Like what, Mom?"

"Jack, do you think Spiderman, when he was little, would treat his mom like you do sometimes?"

Becky knew she had shot way past the point somehow, and Jack's response confirmed it. His howl of violent laughter was followed by, "Good one, Mom!"

Jack's laughter often had a contagious effect on Becky, and that was true this time, although she was still a little peeved at him. "Okay, funny boy—Spiderboy!—get the toys you want for the tub, while I get the bath water the right temperature. If you hurry, I'll let you pour the Spiderman bubble bath into the water!"

Finally, her combined ploys started to work, and Jack got moving collecting toys to take with him into the bubble bath. Surprisingly soon, he came up beside Becky as she was adjusting the water temperature and said, "No one knows how old is God, right, Mom?"

"You're right, Jack; no one does know."

"Mom, I had a dream last night. What do you call those circles around your head, Mom?"

"Crowns?"

"No."

"Headbands? . . . Walkmans?"

"No, Mom. You know those circles around baby's heads?"

"Baby's heads?"

"At Christmas time. You know . . . like in that book."

"What book? . . . Oh, the Leonardo book? The baby Jesus? That's a halo, Jack."

"Yeah! A halo! . . . My halo got as big as a room and then turned into an apple, but I didn't want to go to heaven."

"*Wow!* Why didn't you want to go to heaven?"

"Max says they can walk and talk in heaven. Can they?"

"Nobody really knows, but . . . sure–why not?"

"They're in a case, Mom. They can't stand up."

It finally dawned on Becky that he was talking about a casket, and she said, "They probably walk and talk in heaven, but the best place for a Spiderman bubble bath is here on earth. So, here, start pouring . . . slowly . . . slowly!"

Thankfully soon, Jack's thoughts of death and immortality were submerged in the six-inch suds of the Spiderman bubble bath.

Once the thirty-minute Spiderman bubble bath was over, Jack was refreshed enough to bedevil his mom some more. Having to put on a button-down shirt, and after letting his mom tie his diminutive tie, he complained loudly, looking in the mirror, "It's not *even* cool, Mom. I look like a maniac!" Downstairs, he told his aunt Rachel, concerning the Allison Krause music accompanying the frenzied last-minute Thanksgiving meal preparation, "*Turn it off*! This music makes me sad, like I'm in a desert alone." Of course, the music stayed on, and Jack's button-down shirt and tie stayed on (although the tie was quickly askew). His mother was in too big a rush to give him lessons on life and manners, and her sisters thought he was the cutest thing ever.

For the drinks, Claire had frozen cranberry juice in an ice cube tray. When Jack asked for one of the little popsicles, Claire told him, "It's turkey blood."

Jack exclaimed, "I want some! Mom, let me have some–it's just blood!"

Jack's cousin and schoolmate, Max, said, seeing the huge turkey coming out of the oven, "We had a chicken–that's a turkey! Do you eat the brain? They kill 'em. They put 'em in an oven, cook 'em, and eat 'em!"

Amidst all the hubbub in the kitchen, Jack told his dad that he needed to be, as he put it, "researching the number nine for school–it's homework!" As it turned out, his kindergarten teacher made a research assignment to cut out all the nines they could find in magazines.

Soon after, Jack got yanked up by the biceps and summarily banned from the Thanksgiving meal preparation area when he asked loudly to all present, after the refrigerator kicked on, as it did every few hours, "Why is the refrigerator farting?" And then after a pause for reflection, "Does Grandpa poot?"

Gripping Jack's shoulder and lecturing him in a fairly secluded corner of the living room, Becky looked up to see James, her sister Jill's dapper-looking father-in-law, staring intently at her and her son, hardly a foot away from them. He said to Becky heartily, "Thanks for that announcement!" James had Alzheimer's, and, if she'd had the time, Becky would have worried about the flamboyant and weird mix of people at her Thanksgiving dinner. James just appeared to be warming up, and said, "I don't mean to politicize the situation, but I need to . . . *killer urination!*"

"Oh . . . Mr. Jackson, come right this way," Becky said, guiding him by the elbow to the bathroom. Once she got him to the threshold of the darkened bathroom, he just stood there, embarrassed, and then finally said, "I can't actuate it." Becky turned on the light, guided him physically all the way into the bathroom, and shut the door. "Mr. Jackson, just let us know when you're through. . . ." After quite some time, Becky called through the bathroom door, "Mr. Jackson . . . you doing okay in there?"

Becky could hear quite a bit of fumbling, then, finally, the toilet flushing, but still no James. After a nerve-wracking amount of time, Becky took the plunge and opened the door to find herself standing face-to-face with James, who said apologetically, "I couldn't calm that thing. It was interesting, though." James' bureaucratic vocabulary and problem-solving approach to things made his mental predicament seem all the more incongruous.

Noticing that his pants remained unbuttoned and unzipped and that his belt was twisted into a number of odd and non-functional loops, she said, "Here, let's make some adjustments." With her considerable experience with her granddad and Jack, she quickly got him buttoned, zipped, and properly belted.

"You're ubiquitous! It takes a craftsman to do that!" he exclaimed in genuine appreciation. "Thanks for all your planning. The laughing—the shouting!"

"You're certainly welcome! Let's go see if we can find Jill . . . or Dan." As she led him into the crush of holiday traffic between the living room and kitchen, she noticed he was holding onto the crease in his trousers, right below the pocket, as if he were trying desperately to hold his fragmenting world together physically.

He looked at Becky and asked earnestly, "Will there be anything punitive?"

"No, no . . . no," she assured him, "it hasn't reached that stage yet. For now, everything is just fine. This is a no-fault situation."

By the time the food line began to form at noon and stretch out of the kitchen, Becky was ready to call it a day, although all the preparation had gone well, including the huge, perfectly browned turkey, and Claire's four big pans of homemade rolls. Claire had done artistic little name cards at the place settings to guide guests to their carefully selected spots. However, people ended up moving them around so they could sit where they wanted to, and Becky found herself near the end of the table closest to the kitchen, sitting between her granddad and Mr. Jackson. Very quickly she felt she'd been parachuted into *Alice in Wonderland*, with her grandfather as the Queen of Hearts and Mr. Jackson as the Mad Hatter. Luckily, Jack was tucked away at the children's table downstairs with Claire supposed to be riding herd on him, and Mike was feeding Ruby her ultra-healthy "Zone Diet."

Either gentleman flanking Becky felt perfectly at ease addressing the entire group, anyone in the group, or no one in particular with vehemence and confidence. Her grandfather, precariously waving a full spoonful of marshmallow-topped sweet potatoes to emphasize his points, exclaimed, "Those damned Thermocrats don't give a rat's goll-dang-dolly about anybody. They keep their pants down with no hesitation. Before your very eyes, they'll put their dang-bang butts in a hole in the ground!"

Luckily, no one but Mr. Jackson was close enough to hear the tirade very well, and he responded, "Do you mean that figuratively?" Seeing Becky's granddad's appalled and puzzled reaction, he added, "You're well bent yourself. I'm just saying that I—I do have one *little* sideburn right in the middle of my back. This situation hurts, and I may never dance again."

Getting no verbal response from Becky's granddad, he continued—nervously, rapidly, and steadily—tearing off neat little squares of his paper napkin, "I've always gotten along with the public school system—now I might slip out for a martini now and then. There was no immorality, or anything of that sort—I didn't ride any horses."

Becky's granddad forcefully grabbed her by the arm and leaned in close to tell her in a whisper, "Beck, that man is *completely* screwed and tattooed! If he gives you any trouble, Deb, I can show him the underside of this table, double quick. Just give me the word, babe."

"Granddad, Mr. Jackson is just trying to be friendly," Becky whispered back, aware that Mr. Jackson could hear them.

Interested, Mr. Jackson leaned in close. "Have you met my father?" he asked Becky, implying, she thought, that her granddad *was* his father. "I just cry arms and legs I miss him so much. What a good man, what a succulent gentleman!"

Her grandfather's chin tilted up regally at this string of compliments. Suddenly, all three of them could hear an animated conversation just down from them, with Becky's sister Helen emphasizing, "She does *nothing* but talk about herself!"

Mr. Jackson jumped in with a cavalier rejoinder, "Sounds like my kind of woman!" Later, when someone discussed a serious illness in their family, Mr. Jackson shared some of his family's medical history, saying, "I'm afraid we have blood pressure on both sides of the aisle!"

With her grandfather seated, and the rest of her family responsibilities covered for the moment, getting through the meal was generally pretty easy for Becky, although she jumped up about twenty different times to get someone a fork, or a glass, or a napkin, or a corkscrew—whatever was needed. On one such trip, she looked over the railing to the kids' table downstairs and saw Mike holding court to an adoring group of kids, including Claire, Ruby, and Jack. A few years ago, she would have begrudged the tidal wave of warmth they submerged Mike in when he came back (well, when she allowed him to come back, after kicking him out). Back then he seemed like a politician helped to win a debate because of exceeding miserably low expectations going in (when she seemed to get little credit for her expected backbreaking work every day with her kids). Becky didn't feel that way now. Mike had earned all the love and happiness her kids bombarded him with. She was looking down on his profile, that strong, tan jawline and chin. Ruby was leaning into him, giggling and flapping her hands in glee, Claire had her arm around his neck in a chummy way, and Jack was bouncing around happily on his lap. All their kids had her brownish-black hair. Physically, they made a very interesting picture. Becky never had time or opportunity for such a view. It had an unearthly feel for her, and she heard herself make a sharp intake of breath she was so overwhelmed by the bond she felt for her husband and children. Of course, within seconds, someone was looking for coffee filters, and she was back in the whirl of things.

Becky knew that when you opened your house for such events, you opened your house and took your chances. She was amazed and dismayed, though, that a hearty core of feasters, including Mr. Jackson, still remained at three o'clock. Becky was ready to jump out of her skin by this point. Jack was too old to take naps, so she couldn't use that ploy to clear the house of guests any longer. Finally, as it neared three-thirty, Jill had ushered Mr. Jackson up to the threshold of the front door. He wouldn't commit to taking that final step, though, until he said to Becky, smiling warmly, "You've been so kind. And your children have been so kind. I guess it's the relativity. . . ."

As Jill pulled Mr. Jackson through the doorway, he said, "I was threatened with assassination yesterday."

Becky's granddad clapped Mr. Jackson heartily and warmly on the shoulder and said, "Keep 'er zipped up, bub!" and gave Becky a knowing arch of his eyebrows.

Becky, Mike, and Claire had survived the hard part of Thanksgiving with relatively few problems and no permanent damage, as far as they knew. Three of Becky's sisters were going to watch a movie at one of their houses, but Becky talked them into bringing it over to watch in the finished basement of her house. She was tired of getting left out of so many fun activities because of her care-giving responsibilities. She had read the John Irving novel the movie was based on, and wasn't much worried about showing the movie at her house until it was too late and she read the blurbs on the Blockbuster DVD case: R-rated, "strong sexuality." "Strong" sexuality seemed a bit dicey given the heavy traffic in her house and Jack and her granddad, but there surely must be a way to distract them with other enticing projects or entertainments and to use the remote to click the movie off before either of those two could get a glimpse. Mike's potential reaction worried her, too. He was sometimes unpredictable and volatile in his reaction to things sexual—and that was even before his current problems in that area.

Claire said she wanted to sample the movie to see if she liked it. That made Becky very nervous, but Becky knew that Claire wanted to be a part of the group of grown-up women (as she always had, since she was a little girl). Claire was warned about the spicy nature of the movie, and, as always, advised to leave the moment she felt uncomfortable. Early on in the movie there was quite an extended shot of Jeff Bridges' naked backside as he walked to an outdoor shower. Claire's eyebrows arched to the extent that they seemed ready to take flight. Near the end of that scene, Jack crowed through the high open space that connected the room half a level above to the basement, "Awww . . . big, fat bot-tom!" Claire used this convenient opening to escape gracefully by taking charge of Jack and leading him back to the SpongeBob show he was supposed to be watching.

Becky thought a number of key liberties had been taken with the novel's plot in the movie, and, typically, the sex and romance was glamorized. The forty-year-old woman having the torrid affair with the adolescent Exeter student that summer was much more fit and sexy than the sexy teenaged babysitter. The viewer got a number of extended opportunities to judge exactly how fit and sexy she was. Just at the moment the naked, fit heroine was having sex with her leg nearest the camera extended skyward gymnastically, Becky could hear her grandfather whisper in the dark open corner Jack had peeped through, "Holy burning apocalypse! Mary, Jason, and Jesus!" Before the first half of his exclamation had left his lips, Becky was moving quickly to corral him and head him away, having given up on the movie for good less than thirty minutes into it. As she led her granddad up the stairs to the kitchen, shaking her head in exasperation, those left to enjoy the movie in the darkness below could hear her granddad, stunned and admiring, say, "Deb, that woman was buck, squeaky, totally flaming bum-butt naked!"

Becky couldn't think of much to say to that except, "Granddad, it's just a movie, and it *was* her choice. . . ." Under her breath, she added aloud, "Turn about fair play." She said that in a light-hearted way, but before she had climbed two more steps, the thought took a bitter turn, and she remembered the time she found out Mike had had sex with that nineteen-year-old that worked in his office when Claire and Ruby were babies.

Since Jack and her granddad had been banned from the movie, now probably erupting in overt sexuality in every scene in the darkness below, and since Becky couldn't watch the movie now, she quickly developed a plan to delight and instruct those who had been banished from the movie. Someone always had reading time with Jack before bedtime, and it was most often Becky. Tonight she decided to include her granddad and Ruby, as well. So she gathered up the two peeping Toms and told them her plan as she herded them upstairs. Jack thought the idea was hilarious. "Grandpa at reading time! Awww, Grandpa . . . reading!"

Becky's granddad failed to see the humor in the situation and responded, his feelings wounded, "Jesus Christ in a spoon! I was reading before you or I were born, you little busted barnacle!" Of course, the discussion with Jack about exactly what a barnacle was occupied them the entire trip to his bookshelf.

Jack always got to choose the book for the night, although Becky often tried in subtle ways to sway his choice (and, of course, she oversaw which books he had in the first place). Lately, Jack had been, to Becky's great surprise, extremely interested in the "Getting to Know the World's Great Artists" series. Recently, they had read books from this series featuring the work and life of Toulouse-Lautrec, Van Gogh, Rembrandt, Edward Hopper, and an old favorite, da Vinci. Jack thought the name "Hopper" was really funny for a grown-up artist and showed an especially keen interest in Van Gogh's cutting off his ear (Van Gogh's portrait of himself with his ear bandaged was in the book), commenting, "It looks like he wished he hadn't done it."). A day or so after she read this book to Jack, she was startled by a scream from the kitchen late one afternoon. She rushed in to find Jack holding a paper napkin over his right ear, exclaiming, "I cut off my ear! I cut off my ear!" For a fraction of a second, she was worried that he actually had cut off his ear, then she realized it was an elaborate practical joke and went along with it for a while, to Jack's delight. "Oh, nooo . . . ! Jack, where is your ear? Does it hurt very much? You're going to be so sorry you cut your ear off!"

"Oh, Mom, it's just a joke!"

The two series of books Becky especially pushed were "The World's Great Artists [or Musicians or Authors]" series, which Jack loved since he had begun drawing so much after starting kindergarten, and the "Questions Children Ask About Fill-in-the-Blank (Food, Weather, Nature, Water, etc.)," which Jack wasn't crazy about, although he might, in fact, be interested in some of the questions answered by the books, "Why are pineapples prickly?" "Why is the sky blue?"

Jack was usually quick to choose his book, as if he could spot "Take me! I'm the one for tonight!" written on the cover. Tonight was no exception. He quickly passed over *Curious George Goes to the Aquarium* and even one of his spider books, which almost never happened, and chose the book on Mexican artist Diego Rivera. The cover showed a cartoon figure in a sombrero, sporting bandoliers of bullets, painting one of Rivera's famous murals of Mexican workers. On the cartoon scaffolding upon which he sat were two cartoon cannons and two cartoon pyramids of cannon balls. Becky didn't know if these militaristic touches influenced Jack's pick, but she approved his choice.

Jack had made his choice quickly, but, unfortunately for the harmony of the group, her granddad had made a choice, as well, *Peter in Blueberry Land*. Jack wasn't very thoughtful or kind in his response to his granddad's pick, saying smugly and condescendingly, "Awww . . . *Peter in Blueberry Land*."

Before Jack had even finished, Becky had grabbed his shoulders threateningly and said, "Jack, you need to show your grandpa much more respect!"

Of course, Jack's question, "What *is* respect?" derailed that part of the discussion.

After trying to define "respect" in everyday terms to a macho five-year-old, Becky sought compromise with her grandfather, saying, "Granddad, I'm sure you would enjoy the book on Diego Rivera. He was a great artist from Mexico, and you love Mexico."

His vehement response sent her back-pedaling quickly, "I'm sure I would *enjoy* any number of God-burn-damned things, Beck! But this boy is getting too strong for his ding-bob britches! I do love him, though—I love *all* his toes. I love him to death."

"Well put, Granddad. Okay . . . you both win. . . . We'll read the Diego Rivera book *and Peter in Blueberry Land*. Remember, we're reading these with Ruby, and then you two need to go straight to bed.

Finally settled, sitting of the edge of Ruby's bed, with her granddad on her right, and Jack on her left, and Ruby sitting on her knees behind her left shoulder, Becky explained the situation to Ruby. Ruby was so excited she began bouncing up and down, trampoline-style, as usual, squealing in delight. Soon Becky was leading a rhythmic cheering section, clapping in the old pattern that got Ruby going (two strong, slow claps, followed by three rapid claps), chanting, "Go, Ruby, go! Go, Ruby, go!"

Hearing the commotion, Claire came in and joined the group, climbing up on the bed next to Ruby and, once the bouncing died down, holding one of Ruby's hands while her grandfather held the other, saying, "Sweet, sweet, sweet girl—the sweetest girl . . . sweeter, sweeter, sweeter. . . ."

The book on Diego Rivera claimed, among many other things, "Diego Rivera thought it was important to make paintings for the everyday working people to enjoy. He hoped his art would teach people about their past and give them hope for the future." When her grandfather responded, "Duh . . . !" Becky added the commentary, "Granddad, really powerful art was often for the wealthy few before artists like Diego Rivera."

His response, "Now, Becky . . . I'm not poking a stick in *his* eye . . ." was so inscrutable she just kept on reading. Other highlights of the book included Jack's howl of laughter at Diego looking like a girl in a photograph taken of him as a three-or-four-year-old child around 1890. An ardent communist as an adult, Diego Rivera was from a wealthy family who dressed him up for the photo in a frilly lace dress-like outfit with a ribbon tied in a bow at the waist. However, Jack clearly admired Diego's early approach to art. A two-page color cartoon showed Diego as a child drawing epic scenes of Mexican life all over the walls of his room, the family dog, and his mother's dress while she was still in it. Both Jack and her grandfather were initially speechless at Diego's cubist period in Paris when he was a friend of Picasso. Finally, her granddad said of Picasso's painting of a man with a mustache, buttoned vest and pipe, seated in an armchair, "Looks like a cigar box painted by a drunk drugstore Indian."

Becky responded, somewhat offended by the racist slant of the remark, "Granddad, what do you know about drunken drugstore Indians?"

"Helen," he fired back (Helen was his wife's name), "I know gob-danned enough to invite them to lunch!"

Claire was especially interested in the fact that Rivera was influenced by Italian religious frescoes. She still kept her hand on Ruby's shoulder, although Ruby had long since gone to sleep. Becky's granddad and Jack were mainly interested in the naked breasts of the Indian woman depicted in Rivera's "Creation" mural kneeling on the right side of God, a barrel-chested, round-headed Native American whom both great-grandfather and great-grandson felt must be a professional wrestler. Rivera's portrait of himself with his wife, Frida Kahlo, caused a good bit of animated discussion. Since she was so short compared to Diego Rivera, Jack wanted to know if she were a child. Becky's granddad noted her unibrow and mustache and that her feet were about fifteen times smaller than Diego's.

The next book, *Peter in Blueberry Land*, had such a quaint quality Becky had once checked in the front to see when the book was published. She was only somewhat surprised to find it had first been published in 1901 in Swedish. The quaintness might well have been the reason Becky's grandfather picked the book. In the book, Peter, a boy about eight years old, sets out in the forest to gather a basket of blueberries and a basket of cranberries for his mother's birthday. Peter is sitting in absolute dejection, his head in his hands, after failing miserably to find a single blueberry or cranberry. At this point, he is approached by the king of Blueberry Land, who shrinks Peter down to toy soldier size, like the king, and mobilizes his sons and Mrs. Cranberry's daughters to find the berries Peter needs. Of course, miniaturized Peter gets a remarkable new view of the world on this quest. Mice seem horse-sized and are domesticated to pull blueberry carts; and bees, dragonflies, and spiders are fearsome and huge. As the book ended, with Peter unshrunk, and now in the possession of two baskets of berries for his mother's birthday, Becky's grandfather exclaimed, "Now, that's entertainment!" And no one disputed his claim.

The final phase of getting Jack and Ruby and her granddad to bed wasn't easy, by any means, but when Mike showed up on the scene to take over with Jack, it all went fairly routinely. As her own bedtime approached, Becky began to feel anxious about being with Mike. Their life as husband and wife for over a decade and a half had been an emotional roller coaster and had included Mike's sexual betrayal of Becky and a lack of commitment, from Becky's perspective, to family life. All that led to separation, a slow healing process, and then, miraculously, to the best three years of Becky's life, despite the terrific challenges of caring for Ruby, her granddad, and Jack. Becky felt confident that all women craved and needed tenderness and love as part of sex. She also thought she was probably one of a significant number of women who enjoyed a certain physical power and roughness in sex. Not roughness in terms of enjoying getting hurt, but that feeling that a man simply could not get enough of you and was physically hurling himself, with powerful abandon, inside your very being. Mike was always a great one for raw sexuality, but in recent years his tenderness matched that animal power, and somehow that magnified both qualities.

The last few months, however, Becky watched in horror as Mike completely undercut himself with jealousy. Somehow the jealousy seemed to be born from that perfect happiness they'd had. Becky was the same old Becky she'd always been. She talked to the parents of her children's friends, she talked to the professors and students at the university when she took a class, she talked with people involved in buying or selling her paintings. She knew she was the same old Becky (although her sexual urge seemed stronger than ever), but the supremely confident Mike had become something else. Becky's talking to a young, handsome (yes he was young and handsome, there was no doubt about that) father of one of Jack's friends at the park while the kids played was hardly a good reason for Mike to cut off his penis, but, oddly, to Becky, a few innocent and accidental things like this seemed to have much that effect. Mike seemed to her to create elaborate fantasies about a world full of handsome, talented, youthful, rich, and/or powerful men hatching plots to link up with her, and her with them. Becky, in fact, appreciated handsome, talented, youthful, rich, and/or powerful men as much as the next woman (maybe more), but she had a busy life, she loved her children desperately, and she was in love with Mike, passionately so. In some ways it felt like poetic justice for Mike's behavior early in their marriage. In some ways she would always crave justice from and punishment for that Mike, and she saw to it that he had been well served for many years in that regard. She loved this Mike, and wanted, completely, to see him happy. She wanted to tell Mike that Ted, the handsome young father in the park, seemed far too much like Mike at that age for her to take him seriously in any way.

Although Becky had been anxious about seeing Mike at the end of the day, when she actually saw him, she felt warm and relaxed, and they basically collapsed in each other's arms in their bedroom—and it was only 8:30. They knew that Claire would stay awake up in her room until midnight, and they were relieved that Jack hadn't called out about anything. Becky said, "Thanks for all your help, Mike."

And Mike replied, "Thank *you*, Becky, for all *your* help." It was exactly the right answer, and Becky tightened her embrace, always amazed at the wealth of muscles in Mike's back, arms, and neck. Just like old times, she began to kiss him passionately. And just like old times, he began to kiss her back passionately, and his embrace tightened around her until she felt completely supported, almost suspended in air, by him. In fact, everything seemed like old times, with Mike's sexuality rising on cue to make a triumphant return. Becky felt a huge flood of relief. However, before too long, that powerful rocket of hope and triumph came slowly crashing back to earth. Still in their clothes from the day, Becky sat on the side of the bed with Mike and held him. He said, as if he'd broken a family heirloom, "I'm so sorry, Becky. I'm so sorry. . . ."

A little irritated by his weeks of self-pity, she replied, "There's nothing to be sorry about, Mike. It happens. You'll get it figured out. The doctors will get it figured out. You'll relax about it. You and I will work it out—we will. And if it never works out, fine. That's life. I never thought I'd say this, but you don't need to take yourself so damned seriously. You need to be a man about it!"

When Becky said he needed to be a man about it, she saw a spark of that old terrifying violence (a slight steeling in his eyes and subtle twitch in the muscles in his neck and in his fist) and was shocked that in some ways she was yearning for those old explosive days. Mike never hurt her, but he had always had a magnificent and unpredictable anger, and making up had always been such a sexual catharsis in those days.

Now all he said was, "Becky, you don't know one thing about being a man. You have no earthly idea, and you never will."

"What I think I know, Mike, is that you're doing most of this to yourself. I love you. I love you more than I ever have. I'll love you if we never have sex again." Becky stopped short, realizing that this last point wasn't a good one to make now. They had been over this ground many times in the last six weeks. Even none of the medical remedies seemed to work, and the medical tests revealed no special problems. Becky did all she knew to do. She hugged him and rocked him gently back and forth, sitting there on the side of the bed.

Becky realized that helping the people in her immediate family was, more than anything, what she did now in life, but she couldn't seem to help Mike lately. In fact, anything she might do or say seemed to make matters worse. Mentally, she gave up for a while, but her body kept going on in old familiar ways. She swayed slightly back and forth holding Mike, supporting him in her embrace. Early in their marriage she thought she'd never get over being hurt by him or wanting to hurt him. Now, all she wanted was for him to stop hurting. Hardly realizing it, she began saying, almost to herself, in the rhythm of her movement, tuned with her heartbeat, "You sweet, sweet man," just like she would say, "You sweet, sweet boy," to Jack if she were holding him and he was hurt so badly there was nothing much else to say. Becky caught herself saying this to Mike and jerked slightly, momentarily coming out of her trance. It hit her that Mike might be furious or further wounded by being treated like a child, but she saw in the vacant and stricken look on his face that he seemed beyond caring—a look she'd never seen him have. He looked as if he'd lost every single important thing in his life. Becky continued, unobtrusively, to try to comfort him—or at least be with him in an important way. Tonight, however, his personal devastation would allow for no possibility of a remedy.

The Unheard Music of the Sandwich Generation

Pictograms always annoyed Becky Hawkins far more than she thought they should. She could find no practical, moral, or artistic reason for adults wearing T-shirts that read "I Heart New York" or "I Heart My Peek-a-Poo." However, she wasn't so much annoyed as alarmed in the Abercrombie store in the mall one October morning when she found herself looking over her fourteen-year-old daughter's shoulder into the pictogrammed shirt of a good-looking, long-haired blond boy who looked about seventeen. Becky had always felt that Claire was the soul of innocence, especially for a fourteen-year-old these days. This boy certainly didn't seem to be the soul of innocence; in fact, he even seemed to give Becky a quick appraising glance. He was easily a foot taller than Claire. When Becky had talked to her daughter an hour or so ago, Claire said it was her plan to stay at home and put in a couple of loads of laundry. For safety reasons, Becky needed to know when Claire went places, but now Becky herself felt especially anxious and vulnerable because she had her granddad and Jack in tow. These two were testosterone-saturated time bombs that the monumental two-story high photos of half-naked male teenagers in the Abercrombie and Fitch store could set off any instant (dark-haired Jack actually looked like a seven-year-old version of these models). Her granddad had been riled up the minute they walked in the door and passed the giant bare-chested wash-board-bellied fellow with the zipper on his jeans unzipped and pulling open. Becky didn't think anyone had heard his exclamation, "Buck dang donkey trash!" To which she had heard Jack say, she thought, astounded, under his breath, "Freakin' ass-crack!"

Claire still had her back to her mom and seemed to be talking animatedly to the young guy. Becky's instinct was to jerk her granddad and Jack around and head off the way they'd come before she embarrassed Claire. In one part of her mind she had to admit that Claire seemed to have good taste; the other part of her mind thought that a broken heart (or worse) was in the making for Claire. The young man was handsome and seemed at ease with Claire as he talked to her; at first glance, he didn't seem like some of the macho jerks from high school that Claire could be talking to. Still, as Becky's stare lingered on it, the blue pictogram on his white shirt seemed to demand deciphering. Her granddad and Jack were quiet, for the moment, thumbing through vintage-looking forest-green, maroon, and navy blue and white athletic shirts and jackets. The pictogram was quite a puzzler to Becky. The "I heart" part was easy enough, but then there was a round mirror on a stand (like a make-up mirror), followed by a straight razor like barbers used to use, held by a beaver standing upright, his muzzle lathered thickly in shaving cream, with the beaver poised and ready to shave his huge prickly whiskers (the idea of those oversized whiskers being shaved gave Becky the creeps). Becky struggled with the symbolism of the pictogram . . . "I love mirrors . . . I love straight razors . . . I love beavers . . . I love mirrors, razors, beavers . . . I love mirrors, I love shaving beavers . . . ." It just made no sense to Becky. She puzzled over it for a few more seconds and was ready to make a neat escape with Jack and her granddad, when the pictogram coalesced into its intended meaning for Becky, "I love shaved beaver!" The boy's T-shirt, once translated, cast, in Becky's mind, a much darker picture of her daughter's conversation. Claire had never even been on a date–what was she doing calmly talking with this boy with his smug "I love shaved beaver" T-shirt?

In her haste to leave, Becky grabbed her granddad so forcefully and unexpectedly, he exclaimed over the din in the Abercrombie store, "Dang gob, Becky! Shit on fire! Holy shit on holy fire!" Despite his vehemence, Becky quickly had him turned and heading for the exit, along with Jack. Reflexively, Becky turned and looked back for an instant to assess the damage she might have caused. A weird image flashed through her mind, that of Lot's wife looking back and turning to a pillar of salt in the Bible, only it was Claire who had turned and was frozen in wide-eyed horror and embarrassment, watching her mom, great-granddad, and little brother flee the apocalyptic scene.

Becky was thinking, furious for about fifteen different reasons she couldn't name, that something as simple as slipping into the Abercrombie store at nine-thirty on a Saturday morning to get the raspberry-colored shirt she spotted the other day was an outlandish luxury for her, and next to impossible. Everyone else in the world could saunter in and shop at their leisure, then have a leisurely cup of herbal tea without these two mismatched desperadoes raving and raging in her wake. She had pulled Jack so hard and so fast as she went along, he screamed out, in a weird imitation of her, "Mom, damn it! You stop that right now, or you're in big trouble! *Big trouble!* That's child abuse!" he exclaimed righteously, angry and hurt.

Becky had already gotten out the "God" and was starting in on the "dammit, " having jerked Jack completely off his feet an inch or two, grabbing him under the arm with a violent strength that seemed completely alien to her, when she noticed the dozens of mall walkers zeroing in on her psychodrama (she hated people in the mall who acted like she was acting). She aimed a stage whisper at Jack as they raced along, "Listen, Jack, for someone who just got kicked off of Club Penguin.com for writing the word 'shit,' you–" But looking back at her lagging granddad completely took the wind out of her. The stricken, pathetic look on her granddad's face jarred her out of her anger. He was always ready to spit in the devil's eye and then call him names, but now he looked like a whipped puppy. "Granddad," she said, "what's wrong?"

"Deb . . . Beck–Honey . . . Dang . . . Poop. It's poop. I couldn't. . . ." His usually strong and upright shoulders were slumping miserably.

As the news got worse and worse, the calmer Becky got, the strong gravitational pull of home pulling all three now safely out of the mall . . . slower . . . deliberate . . . steady . . . assured. "Granddad," she said, linking arms with him in a comradely way, "we're going to make it. You're going to be just fine. Even Jack," she said, patting him reassuringly on the head, "is going to be totally, completely fine. We're going to keep walking–don't worry about a thing. There's a towel in the car to sit on. We'll walk through the mall. We'll drive home. We'll get you clean clothes. You watch, within ten minutes you'll be clean and dry, watching TV, sipping hot chocolate with those little marshmallows. Okay?"

"Okay , Helen . . . I could do with some of those little dang bob chains. . . ."

And, not ten minutes later, but thirty, they had achieved those things together, although not one aspect of it was easy. Grown-up poop in a public place had become, after a few unfortunate incidents over the last half year, the thing that Becky feared and despised the most. Changing poop was bad enough any time, but throw in a mortified adult as tall and strong as her granddad and the fact that there was simply no good way to do it, and it became a teeth-clenching, face-flinching exercise of mind over matter. Becky, however, knew that she was good at things like this, compared to most people. She was respectful and calm and determined, and, if it ever came down to it, she was just about as tall and strong and stubborn as her granddad. Once she finished an ordeal like that, she just didn't fret about it any longer.

Now Becky relaxed in the kitchen. She could tell right away what movie it was that Jack and his great-granddad were watching in the living room, drinking their hot chocolate over the coffee table (although drinking and eating in the living room, otherwise, was never, ever allowed). It was a movie Claire and her friends had left in the DVD player after it proved to be a big flop, in their view: *Scary Movie 4*. Becky had initially worried that it was too violent for even Claire and her friends. Claire said it was a total waste of time and money. It wasn't scary at all, it was just dumb–it was just stupid, totally dumb and stupid. Becky, first clearing out some of her e-mail and then cleaning up odds and ends in the kitchen, listened to the movie for signs that it might be too scary for Jack (she didn't have a standard for things being too scary for her granddad). At first on guard, and then intrigued, she kept popping into the living room to watch little snippets of the movie. Immediately, she saw it was a parody of the movie *War of the Worlds*. Becky thought *War of the Worlds* was a dumb movie. She thought this parody was sometimes pretty funny, although the slapstick humor was way "over the top," and it often teetered on the edge of being too much potty humor for her to allow Jack or her granddad, since they could break into this kind of humor at any second of the day, even without encouragement.

Whenever Becky had a spare moment, she tried to answer her e-mails. This morning, there was one aggressive new bidder competing for the right to sell her paintings. Becky did sell her paintings, but, at this point, it was more of a hobby than anything. It seemed to her that this young man, Tony–he might have been no more than twenty-five–was more interested in her than her paintings, although he obviously liked her paintings. Up to this point, she had always gotten along really well with him (maybe too well, she reflected now). He seemed willing to outbid just about anyone, but she knew she didn't want to get entangled in this. Somehow she didn't have the psychic energy to answer his e-mail. After about thirty minutes on her computer and in the kitchen, listening with a small but vigilant censorious part of her mind, Becky decided to relax, drink her chamomile tea, and just let *Scary Movie 4* babysit her two troublemakers. However, it wasn't long until she heard howling laughter from the living room, interspersed with a cacophony of dreadful bathroom noises. Somehow the setting of the movie, as the giant Martian death machines ravaged the countryside, had moved to the temporarily safe haven of a Mennonite or Amish community (surely to be struck with the death rays at any minute). A blind Mennonite maiden, incongruously showing tons of heaving cleavage, had wandered into a Mennonite trial, miraculously thinking it was her own room, and in front of the astonished assemblage proceeded to open a wooden chest, thinking it was some kind of outhouse toilet and then proceeded to discharge an unholy gaseous symphony of supercharged bathroom noises. Jack and his maternal great-grandfather by turns shrieked with laughter and joined in the noise making. As Becky marched righteously toward the Hollywood teenage witches' sabbath unfolding before her ears, she heard the soothing sound of the theme music for the Martian death ray machine. This relaxed her, and she turned back to her tea. She thought she still might actually get to take a little break this Saturday morning. Becky thought that the concept of "sandwich generation" (having elder care and child care responsibilities at the same time) didn't do her domestic situation justice. She would have given anything to have her mom alive to take care of. As it was, her life was an exotic instance of the sandwich generation, the double-decker sandwich generation.

The promotional blurb on the back of her chamomile tea box boasted that the tea was "a soothing antidote for life's complications." That idea always made Becky laugh, but, for the moment at least, life's complications did seem "on hold." Her daughter Ruby's therapist had taken her earlier this morning for an especially long session today—until late afternoon, in fact. Becky still felt a little glow left over from how glad Ruby was to see her when Becky got her ready earlier that morning. Her husband, Mike, was currently doing a monumental list of errands in support of the household. After her tumultuous life of ups and downs with him, she felt the strong magnetic pull of love and sex holding them together in a fierce and wonderful way, whereas, in various ways in the past, it had so often pushed and pulled them apart. It made her shudder to think that Claire was starting out on this road. She hoped that the balance between joy and pain in this part of Claire's life would miraculously tilt to the side of joy without too much unbearable pain preceding it. Becky realized in a panic that her sister Jill was bringing over her father-in-law, Mr. Jackson, for Becky to watch for an hour and feed lunch. With his Alzheimer's at the stage it was, Mr. Jackson presented a challenge for his daily rotating shift of care-givers, and, of course, the wild cards in this particular situation were Becky's granddad, especially, but also Jack.

Luckily, when Jill arrived with Mr. Jackson, Jack was in his room building an elaborate castle with multiple garages and secret chambers out of wooden building blocks, but Becky's granddad was right by her side as she opened the door. Mr. Jackson loved pretty women–well, he loved almost any women—and admired people who seemed to be in control, and Becky was perhaps his very favorite in her large extended family. He had been a bureaucrat who moved in fairly high circles, but was stricken with Alzheimer's right after retirement, or else retired right after he was stricken with it (she didn't know that whole story). He could be condescending to the females taking care of him (mainly his daughters), often referring to them as his "staff," which infuriated them. When he was introduced to Becky, he said gallantly, "Hi, beautiful . . ." and then, dejectedly, forgetting what he was saying, "is it possible for me to elaborate?" He almost jumped back getting a good look at Becky's surly-looking granddad and exclaimed, "That's a *large* virgin!" And then scrambling to be conciliatory, "I'd be glad to give you a lift."

Becky was delighted and shocked to see her grandfather soften at this point. Maybe his humiliation today had given him some perspective and granted him some humility, although she caught the knowing look her granddad gave her, as if to say, "We're going to have our hands full with this character." What he actually said, in a noble and somewhat world-weary way was, "Welcome to my world," and for a weird second it seemed as if he were about to offer Mr. Jackson his elbow so that he could escort him in.

Mr. Jackson returned the courtesy, saying, in his courtly way, "Meo gracias."

Becky and Jill shared a bemused look, and then Jill was off, with Mr. Jackson entering their house confidently, only to proceed to the nearby coat closet, which he briskly entered, closing the door behind him.

Becky quickly opened the door to find Mr. Jackson facing the door calmly, like he was riding an elevator, and it had stopped at his floor. During her few times watching Mr. Jackson, Becky had figured out basic ways of handling him effectively. She grabbed his wrist calmly and confidently and began guiding him to the kitchen, saying, "Let's go into the kitchen, Mr. Jackson, and we'll get your lunch ready. You will love this lunch."

Mr. Jackson replied, "This is Hollywood! This is heaven. We're in good jerky now!" Then, turning to her granddad, he said, "You're very much of a chieftain." When her grandfather didn't reply right away, but shook his head a little sadly, Mr. Jackson continued, "I don't know what the problem is . . . I have a college education."

Luckily, her granddad remained composed and merely exclaimed under his breath, "Sweet Jesus, Jimmy, and James!"

Becky's magic plan for dealing with this situation was to get the two seated and fed before Jack even realized it was lunchtime, but seating Mr. Jackson at the kitchen table quickly turned into an unintended and frustrating slapstick routine. After Becky's fourth attempt to get him seated, Mr. Jackson was standing upright holding the chair against his bottom like his bottom was a head and the chair was a hat. Finally, Becky got him seated well away from the table and managed to push him, with great effort, up flush against the table (narrowly avoiding smashing his hands into the table). She wanted him sitting like this so it would be harder for him to spill his food on his pants and shoes.

Becky quickly put plates down for the two and peeled bananas for each of them to stall them while she fixed the rest of their lunch. She knew they loved bananas, and she knew Mr. Jackson would be ready for his second banana about fifteen seconds after he received his first one. She quickly poured tall glasses of orange juice for each of them, as well, but Mr. Jackson began trying to set his glass on his plate, leaning it perched precariously, slanting as it rested on the rim of the plate. Becky got to the glass before it tipped and fell and placed the glass in Mr. Jackson's hand, which shook noticeably as she and he both held the glass. As she began raising the glass up carefully toward his mouth, against his steady resistance, she said, "Mr. Jackson, why don't you just take the glass and take a drink like this? This is really good orange juice. It's so healthy." She was always astonished at Mr. Jackson's powerful grip. He didn't seem powerfully built, like her granddad, but he clearly had very powerful hands and arms. Once Becky got the glass to his lips, he easily followed through and began drinking, drinking half the tall glass at the very first go, and then finishing the rest just as quickly.

Her granddad was impressed and exclaimed jovially, "Where's the Dang Gob outhouse fire, bub?"

Mr. Jackson replied not to her granddad but to her, "That was moisture-ous! That's love! Ah, that was felth and fucker . . . Pardon my French! Could you bring me another . . . at your convenience?"

With that, Becky's granddad ominously screaked his chair back slowly and stood up threateningly over Mr. Jackson, saying, "Listen, young fella, you come under this roof, you come into this room, you sit on this table . . . you better zip your Gob Rotten Dang mouth up, you better zip your flamin' pants up, you better zip your holy ass up, sit on the pot, or blamin' get out!"

As Becky prepared to intercede, she said, "Granddad, you know Mr. Jackson needs our help. . . ."

Mr. Jackson seemed both contrite and bemused, chuckling at how easy it seemed for people to misunderstand his intentions. "No . . . no . . ." he said apologetically, "people seem to think there's a growing . . . faxtail. No . . . no . . . I believe in the softness . . . in the hills. I'm not inviting that special bubble." And then Mr. Jackson's face scrunched into an agony of thought, and after a long silence, he continued thoughtfully, "Scrivermus, scioto . . . telemans . . ." To which he added when there was bewildered silence, "Just kidding." Then he turned sensitively to Becky's granddad and said, "You having marital problems?"

To which her granddad replied, "Well, this morning, I lost it in the dad gang mall. Quite a total flaming mess. But Deb here– Becky–is a good girl–quite a woman, you know. We will not see her like again."

As peace reigned, Becky hurried to fix her granddad a bowl of Contadina brand minestrone (it was a pretty healthy soup for a soup in a can) and to fix Mr. Jackson a toasted peanut butter and strawberry jam sandwich, fixed so that no peanut butter or jam would leak out. She had learned the hard way that she could fix almost no other meal that he could handle. He would try to eat potato chips with a fork. He would do unspeakable things with anything in a bowl. He could hardly handle any regular food cut up on a plate. If you got him something like a Whopper with cheese from Burger King, you might as well open it and apply it directly to his face, shirt, and hands.

Becky had transferred Mr. Jackson's sandwich successfully to his right hand, and he was eating it proficiently (chomping voraciously and quickly, completely down one row, and then the next). Becky was always afraid he was going to get a bite of her finger in the transfer. By now her granddad's soup was nearly heated and ready when Jack came bounding in and gave his granddad a big hug from the back, around and over the chair. Becky sighed to herself, realizing the Testosterone Twins were back in action.

Although Jack could be a sensitive and loving boy, and certainly was a smart and artistic boy, he was right at the 100-percent range on the rowdy, loud, macho scale. He still could hardly walk through a room without hitting, kicking, elbowing, karate-chopping, jumping out at, leaping on everything, both inanimate and human, in his vicinity. That is, he acted this way when he was alone with his family. She had long ago learned that he was the perfect, thoughtful gentleman at school, and it infuriated Becky that he could turn his obnoxious behavior on and off. She realized that their life was chaotic by nature, and she was too busy to be perfectly consistent in shaping and controlling his behavior, and this was a good example of such a time. Mr. Jackson, her granddad, and Jack basically each required the full-time attention of one adult to be properly watched over (if Ruby were home, that would be four in that category). Luckily for Becky, Mike had become great at this kind of care over the last four years or so, and Claire was becoming a great help, too, although Ruby and her granddad were too much for Claire to control physically, and Jack was almost in that category, as well.

Jack was actually very shy around people he didn't know, so he had sidled up to his granddad and was trying to talk to him out of earshot of Mr. Jackson, but Becky could see Mr. Jackson listening intently. As his granddad was spooning in the minestrone with gusto and determination, Jack was firing off a string of questions and statements about war (and an occasional one about rock and roll). "Granddad, did you use a flamethrower in war, or a grenade launcher, or a bazooka?" "Is Mexico good at war, or do they suck at it?" Becky was going to jump in and say, "Don't say words like 'suck.' You need to watch what you say." But just at that point her granddad calmly responded, "They suck at it, bub." Becky decided that this was not a good "teaching moment" to discuss the horrors of war with Jack or how he should speak, in public or elsewhere. Jack continued excitedly–he and his granddad talked like this all the time– "Granddad, are you born with no clothes on? Can you be born in a war? I don't want to be born in a war." "All my friends say machine guns are how you kick major butt." "War is fun, but it's not good to kill people. [Becky knew Jack was playing to her now.] I like war–I *really* like war– but I never want people to die in war."

On that note, Mr. Jackson chimed in, trying to speak around the impressive amount of peanut butter and toast in his mouth, "Ah . . . we . . . we . . . ah . . . um, this is pungent, and–what's the word– smarmy. . . ." Becky gave him a small glass of water, which he promptly chugged straight down. Then he made his long-sought observation, "We like to see people die . . . we just don't like to see people get hurt." In the brief silence that followed, everyone seemed to acknowledge that statement as true and profound, so that Mr. Jackson's follow-up comment was lost on all but Becky, "At least, I know I do." And then quietly, "Getting circumsized– that's nothing to laugh about . . . not if you're Catholic."

Jack was off again, "Granddad, is a mosh pit the most dangerous place in the world?"

To which his granddad replied, both sternly and kindly, "You wash your mouth out, son. You're big enough to be potty-trained."

"No, Granddad, they throw bottles and stuff while the band plays up front–those metal bands. Sam's dad told him all about it. He nearly got killed in a mosh pit." For the last month, Jack had been intrigued about the exotic dangers of the mosh pit. Mike had told him, when Jack kept asking him about it, how wild teenagers used to drink alcohol down front by the band and slam into each other and throw beer bottles (it was the thrown beer bottles that nearly killed his friend's dad). A few weeks ago after a picnic Becky and Mike had in the back yard, Jack was collecting beer bottles, which he had lined up neatly in a row on the driveway in the back. He told Becky, proudly pointing to his beer bottle collection and using his ironic tough-guy voice, "I'm goin' to the mosh pit!"

The greatest thing that happened for Becky during Mr. Jackson's stay is that he didn't need to go to the bathroom (at least that she knew of). She had helped him go before, and she knew basically that he was beyond help in this area. He couldn't go by himself, and he couldn't be helped to go. The best that could be done is that the mess be minimized and that then he be cleaned up. Becky felt that she had had her quota of that activity for this day, and was delighted that she escaped unscathed with Mr. Jackson. As Jill came to get him and take him home for the afternoon, he turned to Becky's family and said in a chipper way, "Well, it's been smartingly smart . . . no, I mean it. . . . I gotta go get crucified."

As Jill maneuvered Mr. Jackson out the door, the family cat, Toto, used the opportunity to sneak in, and right behind Toto was Mike, carrying about eighty pounds of groceries suspended from his hands in eight or so bulging plastic bags. Mike always calmed Jack and Becky's granddad considerably; he was a strong physical presence, but somehow it was his sympathetic but no-nonsense approach in recent years that calmed these two down the most. Mike was hugging Becky in that way that took forever and that the family members had grown to expect, with wry smiles and much rolling of the eyes from the kids, when the phone rang in the kitchen. As usual, everyone just waited for the message. "Hi, Becky, this is Tony. You know, since I didn't hear back from you this morning, maybe the best plan is to discuss this over a coffee at the Hazelwood this afternoon, or sometime soon. . . . Well, you know where to find me. . . . Talk to you soon."

Becky watched that old dark look from yesteryear mask Mike's face, right as Claire zipped through the living room, giving her mom an assessing look that Becky couldn't decipher. Becky was still in Mike's embrace, which had gone somehow both limp and tense. She gripped his strong shoulders as she assessed his mood. He said, some of the sting gone out of his look, "Becky, who is that young guy? Was he calling for Claire or for you?" and then, as a joke, which was a very good sign, "And where does he live?"

Becky relaxed some, and said, "He wants to sell those four paintings. The 'Summer' series. His price is good, but something isn't quite right. I'm not going to do it."

Becky and Mike used the tag-team approach to child-rearing and elder care throughout the day. Once the groceries got put away and everyone had eaten, Becky ended up with Jack, and Mike ended up with Becky's granddad. With less than two weeks to Halloween, Jack was obsessed with choosing the perfect costume, or, it seemed to Becky, to connive as many costumes or accessories as possible from her in the mad rush to Halloween itself. He already had a costume he called "The Scream." To Becky the mask seemed directly patterned after painter Edvard Munch's painting of the same name. For Jack, however, the costume was inspired by the murderer in the first *Scary Movie*, who wore such a mask. Becky had no idea when Jack had seen such a movie. Jack was hinting around that he wanted to consider alternate costumes. "Mom," he said, "would you rather be a pirate, or a knight, or a Viking?"

"Jack," Becky answered, "Pirates, knights, and Vikings had absolutely no good parts for women, but I want to show you where your Scream costume came from . . . I found it in an old art book I have."

Jack seemed interested enough. She had continued to read with him a number of "The World's Greatest Artists" series books for kids (Leonardo da Vinci, Rembrandt, Picasso, Diego Rivera, and Edward Hopper remained favorites, but they had no Edvard Munch). She found a photo of the painting in an old art history book of hers. As they sat on the couch with Becky thumbing through the book to find the right plate, Jack tried to put his arm around Becky's neck. His arm only reached high enough to nestle at her neck. Becky loved this side of Jack, a side that was usually short-lived before bursting into some sort of robust, loud, and probably dangerous behavior. Sometimes he seemed to Becky only to have inherited the negative traits from both her and Mike, but none of their positive traits. Becky knew that that wasn't true, and moments like this, which happened a time or two every day, helped remind her. When Becky found the painting "The Scream," Jack was astonished. "When did *they* see the movie!" he exclaimed.

"Jack, the movie got the idea from the painting–it's famous. The costume makers got the idea from the movie."

"Mom, where's that bridge 'The Scream' is standing on?"

"Jack, the painter was Norwegian, it says. It could have been a bridge in Norway he knew, or he could have just made it up. It's a painting, Jack, not a photograph. Look, you can't even tell if the screamer is a man or a woman."

"Whoa, Mom, that's crazy. . . ."

"The point is that whoever that is is screaming with everything that's in them. Whatever it is they're screaming about must be pretty bad."

"You got that right, Mom," said Jack, impressed. "This is a *great* costume!"

Becky was of the "plate spinning" school of child rearing and elder care. Like that act in the circus in which one harried performer kept fifteen plates spinning on the top of fifteen sticks. She had Jack and her granddad spinning successfully, and Ruby wouldn't be back for thirty minutes or so, so she sought out Claire. She didn't find Claire at the computer or watching either of their TVs or in her room or eating in the kitchen, but she did find her doing laundry in the basement. Becky paid her to wash, dry, and fold five loads each week, while Becky did the other five loads (Mike's rotation into this chore had been short-lived and unsuccessful). Once again Becky found herself, unobserved, observing her daughter from behind. She was a beautiful, calm, thoughtful girl, and although she had the same black-brown hair as Jack, she was his polar opposite. It didn't seem long ago to Becky that Claire was Jack's age and thought Oprah Winfrey had given her name to her favorite dish, fried "Oprah."

Claire jumped, startled, when she finally sensed her mom behind her. "Mom," she said, "you've got to stop sneaking up on me. . . . What was up with you and granddad and Jack this morning?" . . . Claire continued to move sopping wet clothes from the washer to the dryer as she talked. . . . "Dylan thinks I have the weirdest family . . . but he thinks you're all kind of cute, in a weird sort of way."

"Claire," Becky said, already relieved at the vibes she was getting from Claire, "with that T-shirt he had on, he has a lot of nerve thinking we're weird. . . . That shirt could certainly seem insulting to some women."

"Mom, he just wears that shirt to be funny. He's a funny guy. He really is."

"Claire, you need to be careful with guys that age . . . well, with any guys . . . you're just so inexperienced. Does he like you? Does he want to go out with you? Claire, it's so easy to really get hurt badly in these things?"

Claire started the dryer, turned to her mom, and then began to try to talk over the dryer, "Mom, I'd give anything if he liked me . . . well, he *does* like me. He's got Ashley, Mom. It doesn't seem easy for girls like Ashley to get hurt in things like this . . . just me. . . . They're all having a great time. I'm the only girl without anyone."

Becky, who was now hugging her daughter comfortingly, had not expected any part of this conversation to go the way it had. "Claire . . ." she sighed, "if you get someone half as good as you, you'll be the happiest girl in the world?" Becky realized that the "birds and the bees" part of this discussion would have to wait. She was getting choked up, and Claire was sobbing quietly on her shoulder.

Later, when Becky went to look out the front window to see if the therapist was coming with Ruby, she thought it would be a funny scene if Dylan ever showed up to one of her extended family's get-togethers (she had some pretty conservative older relatives). The therapist was nowhere in sight as Becky scanned down the street, but she did see Mike, Jack, and her granddad playing basketball at the goal in their back driveway. It was such an idyllic scene. Jack was a whirling dervish, racing endlessly, shooting or chasing the ball with his dad. Always, when alone with Jack, her grandfather was like a perimeter-trained Rottweiler, protecting him, keeping him safe, keeping him away from the street and front walk. But with Mike around, he could relax and play a little himself. The goal had been lowered to eight feet for Jack, and she could hear Jack's squeal of approval as his granddad dunked the ball virtually flat-footed.

When the therapist brought Ruby home, Becky carefully navigated her up their front steps and then up the stairs to the second-floor, where all the bedrooms were. This was always quite a maneuver because Ruby was such a big girl and needed careful help and support with each step to avoid falling. Even a slight misstep sent her into an agony of panic. Throwing Ruby off, as Ruby pulled automatically towards her own bedroom, Becky took her straight to her and Mike's bed. Claire had been planning for a long time to paint Ruby's fingernails, and maybe toenails, and Becky had decided to help as long as peace reigned in the household. Claire at first thought she would use bubblegum pink, then she leaned towards the metallic ruby-flake color of Dorothy's slippers in *The Wizard of Oz*, but, finally, she settled on black, a tribute to the new style and Ruby's advance toward her teenage years, but also because of Halloween and to match the shirt she was wearing, which Claire had picked out for her. It featured a stylish pirates' skull and crossbones, with one of the front teeth in the skull capped in gold. "Ruby," Claire told her sister, "you're going to be completely stylin'."

Becky added, "Ruby wants to look grown up now that Claire has picked out all her cool new clothes. All those boys on the bus and at school think Ruby is just too cute." Ruby was flapping her hands so hard in ecstasy and squealing so hard, Claire had to wait a long time for Ruby to calm down. Among many other things, it was clear now that Ruby would never talk. She wasn't happy that many times a day, but when she was, she expressed it in very clear and vigorous physical ways. What she loved were the sound of her mother's and father's voices and the sound of Jack getting in bad trouble (well, she generally enjoyed anyone having obvious trouble), and she loved her parents and sister bragging about her. Those things tickled her and delighted her just about every time.

Claire put on her music, and a rap song was playing when Mike, Jack, and Becky's granddad walked in. The female rapper was expressing something like, "Every time you come around, my London, London Bridge wanna go down." Jack was leading his granddad, holding his hand to guide him, but he was asking his dad, "Dad, when germs go down the drain, do they like it?"

"Well, Jack," his dad said, "I suppose it depends on who you ask. We don't really know how much germs think. Or how they think. Some germs probably like it okay, and some probably don't. The kid germs probably like it, and the parent germs probably say, "Don't do that . . . stop . . . come back . . . !"

Becky wagged her index finger at the male half of the family and said, "This is a quiet, calm zone. Anyone who isn't quiet and calm has to leave, okay, Jack?"

"Mom," Jack said, crawling up on the king-sized bed with his sisters and mom, "I'm not being mean."

Astonishingly, both Mike and Becky's granddad sat down on the bed, as well. And then Mike began rubbing Becky's shoulders. Becky always believed, theoretically, in the concept of the "family bed." In theory, to her it seemed a healthy follow-up to breast feeding, but the breast feeding was as far as she ever went. Parents needed some time to recuperate each day. They needed some time to themselves. Kids didn't need to control even the parents' bed. Of course, the average age of this family in the bed was around thirty years old. In all her life as a grown up this had never happened with her family, although this kind of scene seemed pretty typical with Becky's mom and all of Becky's sisters and brothers growing up. For the last several years, Becky had been waiting, on a daily basis, for the next of a life-long series of disasters to strike (not that they didn't already have a lifetime supply). *Well,* she thought, Mike's backrub easing her up to the verge of sleep, *it hasn't happened yet—but the day's not over.* That's at the point when she felt Jack's hand softly kneading her upper arm in a clumsy imitation of his dad. The last thing she heard before she dozed off a bit was her granddad chuckling, "Well, it beats a firecracker up the wazoo!" Or, was she dreaming that?

It didn't happen often, but maybe once or twice a month, Becky and Mike paid Claire to babysit while they went out. They always got Ruby ready for bed and in bed, Becky's granddad ready for bed and in bed, and Jack at least headed the direction of bed before they left. They were going to a restaurant called Blaze, and Claire had Becky's cell phone number and the restaurant's telephone number, in case anything happened. A steakhouse wasn't Becky's first pick in a restaurant usually, but she and Mike did both want to try this new place. It was actually a pretty good place, they both agreed, and since they started with Tanqueray and tonics and proceeded to Cabernet Sauvignon with the meal, their cares were melting away as the meal progressed. Becky almost felt like a high school girl on a date . . . well, in terms of how giddy she felt. She felt the opposite of a high school girl on a date, given her total lack of anxiety. It was a good place, but they took themselves a little too seriously in the steakhouse department. When the waiter initially came out, Becky thought it was the owner or chef, given his chef's hat, but at some point she noticed all the waiters dressed like that. When Mike's baked potato was delivered, the waiter wheeled out a huge copper cart topped with condiments in silver bowls. The waiter gave a "voilà" motion toward the cart and said, "And for your potato pleasure . . .?" Something about this cracked Becky up. She managed to keep from giggling aloud, but, under the table, she grabbed Mike in a favorite tender spot. Mike let out a choked peep before he regained his dignity a little and said to the shocked waiter, "Ah . . . chives, bacon, and butter . . . ."

Later, Becky and Mike decided to walk around town a bit after they finished their meal, which they did, leaning on each other in a chummy and flirty way. When they finally got to their car, parked at the far extreme of a vast series of downtown parking lots, Mike said to Becky, "Maybe Jack's not even in bed yet. If Claire hasn't put him to bed yet, it's going to take *forever* to get him in bed." Not having to put Jack to bed was one thing both Becky and Mike prized at night. Another thing they prized was their privacy, to talk and/or have sex at night. They went to bed early and got up early, and this type of privacy was at a premium for them in their house. Their car was really one of those souped up new types of vans, but it had even less room in the front seat than most cars and more space for the stick shifter. One thing led to another between Becky and Mike. This was really a first for Becky. She had never had sex like this in a car as a teenager or young adult, or ever. And she certainly never imagined that she and Mike could twist into the positions they did, but they both were highly motivated, and, before long, satisfied. Becky was necessarily the last to be satisfied, and just as she was becoming completely satisfied, she could hear her cell phone ringing. Of course, she didn't care if it rang or not through the first few rings, then, as her more normal feelings ebbed back into her body, she realized the ringing was coming from Mike's pants pocket. She had given him the phone to carry earlier since she had no good place to carry it. Mike was in a very awkward position to retrieve the phone efficiently. Becky and Mike both grappled in the ringing pocket, trying not to hurt Mike, currently in a vulnerable position anatomically, in the process.

Finally, Becky managed to get the phone extracted, knowing it was Claire, and hoping the trouble wasn't too bad (Claire wouldn't be calling if the trouble weren't fairly bad). Becky's sense was right, and Claire exclaimed in exasperation, "Mom, where have you been!? You said you'd be home by 9:15! Jack was awful. He was *so* bad. He hit me for no reason. He was a monster—the worst he's ever been. He jumped off the stairs and landed on my foot. I think my toe might be broken—"

Becky broke into Claire's frantic catalogue of babysitting problems, "Claire, I'm so sorry. The time just sort of got–"

"Mom, I know granddad's up. I can hear him in there. I think he might have had some trouble going to the bathroom or something."

"Claire, I'm so sorry. . . . We'll be right home. We'll make it up to you. We can get your foot checked out, but the doctors can't do anything for a broken toe. All the other times you thought you broke a toe or finger you were fine."

"Mom," Claire said, finally cheering up a bit, "you're grounded!"

Becky could see Mike watching her, bemused, still in what was to Becky a provocatively disheveled state. Apparently, he could tell by listening to and watching her that there was no real crisis. After Becky had finished talking to Claire, Mike said to Becky with a smirk, "Shaved beaver is sweet, but unshaved beaver sweeter." She and Mike had talked at dinner about the T-shirt of the boy talking to Claire. Becky thought such pandering to men, such shaving, held nothing for women, and therefore was somewhat demeaning. Mike seemed to have a completely open mind on the subject. Becky was somewhat shocked at what Mike said, not the shaved beaver part, but the way he said it seemed clearly to be an allusion to poetry, British Romantic poetry. That didn't especially seem like Mike, but he had been full of surprises, in her view, lately. As Becky and Mike made themselves presentable again, Becky tried to remember the exact part of the poem Mike alluded to. Was it "Ode to a Grecian Urn"? Was it "heard music is sweet, but unheard music sweeter"? That poem was by Keats . . . or was it Shelley?

On the ride back home, both Becky and Mike were calm and content, although Becky knew they would have their hands full for awhile once they got back home. Becky sensed a breakthrough tonight with Mike. In some ways it had happened years before when she let him come back home, but in the back of her mind she had still worried. They had had some miserable, awful, terrible years together, along with the exquisite years, and the years just coasting along (well, their relationship was coasting–since Ruby, their lives had always been an indescribable struggle). Becky had never really thought people could change fundamentally, but it seemed obvious to her Mike had. She had insisted Mike change, and somehow he did. And he did it in a way in which he was even truer to himself. At a certain point in life, the fiercely competitive nature of males just made no sense, in human terms. Becky realized that part of what fed her fury, off and on, all those years, was that Mike was much more than he was to her. Now, somehow, they had come to a silent agreement to share themselves fully, and, after a life of incredible hardship, that created a feeling that was intensely sweet.

www.ingramcontent.com/pod-product-compliance
Lightning Source LLC
LaVergne TN
LVHW091225080426
835509LV00009B/1175